Freedom to Believe

Freedom to Believe

Patrick Sookhdeo Ph.D., D.D.

Freedom to Believe

Published in the United States by Isaac Publishing
6729 Curran Street, McLean VA 22101

Unless otherwise stated, all Qur'anic references are taken from A. Yusuf Ali's *The Holy Qur'an: Text, Translation and Commentary,* Leicester: The Islamic Foundation, 1975. They are given as the *sura* (chapter) number followed by the number of the verse within the *sura*. Verse numbers may vary slightly between different translations of the Qur'an, so if using another version it may be neces-sary to search in the verses just preceding or just following the number given here to find the verse cited.

Library of Congress Control Number: 2009934075

ISBN 978-0-9787141-9-2
Printed in the United States of America

Contents

Foreword by Bishop Michael Nazir-Ali. 7

Introduction. 13

1   What Classical Islam Teaches about Apostasy 15

2   Muslims Debate and Interpret the Apostasy Law 41

3   The Application of the Apostasy Law in the World Today 55

4   Conclusion 99

    Appendices

    Apostasy: Major and Minor (Yusuf Al-Qaradawi) 101

    Freedom of Religion in Islam (M.A. Zaki Badawi) 119

    Universal Declaration of Human Rights 129

    Cairo Declaration on Human Rights in Islam 137

    Glossary 145

    Endnotes 149

    Index 163

Foreword:
Apostasy and Blasphemy in Islam:
What Should Christians Do?

The Qur'an is fierce in its condemnation of apostasy (*ridda*) and of the apostate (*murtadd*). Theirs, according to it, will be a dreadful penalty (*'adhāb*^{un} *'azīm*^{un}). This sentiment, which occurs in *Sura* 16:106, is re-expressed in other ways in other *suras*. The interesting point to note is that the various threats of judgement and of punishment seem to relate to the next world or to life after this earthly one, rather than to this world and to this life.

Against this, we have the unanimous position of the various schools of Islamic law (*fiqh*) that shari'a lays down the death penalty for adult male Muslims in possession of their faculties who apostatise. Some schools also prescribe a similar punishment for women, whilst others hold that a woman apostate should be imprisoned until she recants and returns to Islam. In addition to this, should an apostate somehow escape the ultimate penalty, his property becomes *fai'*, i.e. it becomes the property of the Muslim community, which may hand it over to his heirs; his marriage is automatically dissolved and he is denied Muslim burial.

How then did such a major difference arise between the *prima face* teaching of the Qur'an and the provisions of shari'a as codified by the various schools of law? The answer is that the death penalty for apostasy is to be found in the *hadith*, the various collections of traditions about the Prophet of Islam's sayings and doings, and it is also found in the *sunna* of Muhammad and of his closest companions, the reports about their practice.

Commentators on the Qur'an, both ancient and modern, sensing this tension, have attempted to find passages that could be interpreted as teaching the death penalty for apostates. Thus 2:217, which speaks of the barrenness of an apostate's life and work, in both this world and the next, is interpreted as meaning that apostates will be punished both in this world and in the next. Similarly, passages such as 4:88-89 are taken as justification for inflicting capital punishment on apostates.

On the other hand, there are those who take as their point of departure the Qur'anic silence on penalties in this world for apostasy. They either minimise the force of the traditions that require it or reject them altogether. It is said, for example, that the traditions that speak of the death penalty for apostates are weakly attested or from an unreliable source. If they contradict the Qur'an they are to be rejected as an accurate account of what Muhammad may have said. They are also to be rejected if they do not cohere with other accounts of his behaviour or speech.

Others point to the supposed practice of the second Caliph 'Umar, who disliked the extreme penalty for apostasy and was followed in this by some of the early *fuqaha* or lawyers. More recently, this view has gained currency in some circles close to Al-Azhar As-Sharif, the premier place for Sunni learning, located in Cairo, Egypt. According to these scholars, the traditional time given to an apostate to repent must be extended to the whole of his life.

Many scholars claim that the punishment for apostasy in the time of the Prophet and of his Companions arose because rejection of the Islamic faith was linked to rebellion against the nascent Islamic state. So the punishment was not so much for apostasy as for treason. The well-known scholar, Sheikh Qaradawi, whose opinions are widely studied and followed, relying on the medieval jurist and reformer Ibn Tamiyya, distinguishes between the greater and the lesser apostasy. The lesser apostate, whilst being subject to civil penalties, would not be put to death but those who proclaim their apostasy, thus destabilising Islam and the Muslim *umma* (or nation), would be. This may be a useful distinction to make but is hardly a manifesto for freedom of expression or of belief.

Although apostasy is punishable by death in only a few countries, such as Saudi Arabia, Yemen and Sudan (Iran seems to be drawing back from putting it on the statute book, at the time of writing), in fact jurists will sometimes directly invoke the authority of shari'a to sentence apostates to death. This has happened in both Iran and in Afghanistan. In addition to judicial process, those accused of apostasy can be killed in prison, through torture or poisoning, or by mobs attacking their home or place of work, or even by relatives!

Whilst apostasy, and its penalty, are applicable to Muslims, the offence of *Sabb*, of insulting the Qur'an or the Prophet of Islam, can also be applied to non-Muslims. Blasphemy against the Prophet is punishable by death, though the method of execution varies from one authority to another. It is this that led the Federal Shari'a Court in Pakistan to rule out any other penalty but death for blaspheming Muhammad. The so-called "Blasphemy Law" has caused considerable grief for Christians and other non-Muslim minorities since even the expression of their belief can be construed as insulting the Prophet. The Law has also become a way of settling personal scores by accusing one's adversary of blasphemy. There have been numerous convictions in the lower courts, though fortunately the higher courts have invariably, so far, overturned these verdicts. In the meantime, the family is left destitute and the community from which the accused comes left vulnerable to harassment and intimidation.

The irony is that Muslims claim that their prophet forgave those who insulted him and there are a number of stories to this effect in the *sira* (life of Muhammad) and in the *hadith* (there are also other stories that describe how those who insulted him were punished). Which of these attitudes is to prevail in contemporary Muslim societies?

A number of administrative and judicial attempts have been made to ease the lot of those accused of blasphemy and to make it more difficult to file charges of blasphemy against someone. None of these has been wholly successful. The law returns again and again to haunt the political establishment and the judiciary. The only solution is for a government to have the courage to repeal it or to abolish or suspend the death penalty altogether, thus leaving other penalties for dealing with alleged cases of "insulting religion" or blasphemy, as indeed existed before the current law was promulgated. Some of the *'ulama* are bound to object to such steps, if the government takes them, and there may well be "popular" movements to resist the repeal or amendment of the law. Such resistance needs to be faced down and genuine objections, such as the claim that Islamic law prescribes *qisas* or retaliation for murder and that therefore the relatives of the murdered person have the right to seek life for life, or alternatively compensation, will have to be met. It is already the case that *qisas* cannot be carried out by an individual or group but must be left to the state. If the death penalty were to be abolished or suspended for all serious crime, could not the state order and enable compensation to be paid instead of the death penalty as part of its judicial and executive responsibility? These issues need further exploration but it is clear that the present blasphemy law is neither just nor compassionate and needs to be dealt with while there is opportunity.

Most Muslim countries have subscribed to international treaties, such as the UN Declaration of Human Rights, but they subordinate such agreements to the provisions of the shari'a, which, in many cases, negates the effect of these documents. In this connection, it is interesting to compare the UN Declaration with the Cairo Declaration on Human Rights in Islam. In the latter there is no equivalent to Article 18 (on freedom of thought, conscience and religion) of the former and all provisions are, ultimately, subject to shari'a. This approach has resulted, again and again, in important rights under Article 18 of the UN Declaration being denied to people in Islamic countries on the grounds that they contravene the provisions of shari'a. This situation has caused much frustration to human rights activists, constitutional lawyers and even progressive regimes as any provision in law can always be trumped by an appeal to shari'a.

If the impasse created in this way is to be avoided, it is necessary for leading institutions in the Islamic world to undertake a major reform of shari'a so that the principles of amelioration and of movement, which exist in at least some of the *madhahib*, or schools of law, are not only recognised but actually acted upon in both religious and other courts, as there is need. There is also, of course, the urgent task of *ijtihad*, i.e. a fundamental examination as to how the principles of law to be found in the Qur'an and other sources of Islamic law can be brought into a fruitful relationship with present-day conditions and requirements. This is the case, for example, in the areas of finance, family law, penal provisions, jihad and the treatment of non-Muslims in an Islamic state.

Christians, of course, in the context of dialogue with Muslims and with Islamic religious and political authorities, will encourage those who are struggling to maximise fundamental freedoms in Islamic contexts. They will also be active in advocacy for those who have fallen foul, both materially and spiritually, of traditional understandings of laws and customs regarding apostasy and blasphemy. It remains important to raise awareness of what is happening in so many parts of the world so that people can learn from, pray for and give to those who have become victims of these draconian laws and customs.

The book that follows considers, within a short space and very read-ably, how the penalties for apostasy arose within Islam and how they were implemented. It considers the different responses to the laws in the early period, by various reformers and also in our own times when the issue has, once again, become a live one. The appendices are valu-able in providing material from contemporary eminent Islamic scholars and also the text of both the UN Declaration of Human Rights and the Islamic Declaration. Dr Sookhdeo has provided an important hand-book for all those who care about and deal with the issue of fundamen-tal freedoms. Many will be grateful to him for this timely volume.

+Michael Nazir-Ali
July 2009

The Rt Revd Dr Nazir-Ali was until recently Bishop of Rochester.

Introduction

Everyone has the right to freedom of thought, conscience and religion; this right includes freedom to change his religion or belief, and freedom, either alone or in community with others and in public or private, to manifest his religion or belief in teaching, practice, worship and observance.[1]

United Nations Universal Declaration of Human Rights

We always remind those who want to convert to Islam that they enter through a door but there is no way out.[2]

Kuwaiti jurist, speaking in 1996

On 4 June 2009 Barack Obama, President of the United States, gave a keynote speech in Egypt on American relations with the Muslim world. Shortly before his visit, the Sheik of the prestigious Al-Azhar mosque extended an invitation to the president to use it as the venue for his address. Mohammed Sayyed Tantawi said that a speech from the mosque could "open the door for a dialogue of reason between the world's cultures and civilisations to spread values of justice and good against hatred and violence." The speech was eventually given at Cairo University, but the invitation was significant in itself.

Barack Obama's late father and grandfather were Muslims, but the president himself is a professing Christian. According to Islamic shari'a law, the child of a Muslim parent is to be regarded as a Muslim, regardless of the other parent's faith. So by embracing Christianity Obama has made himself an "apostate" in the eyes of Islam; that is, he is someone who has abandoned Islam, and as such under shari‘a he deserves the death penalty.

The invitation extended to the president to speak at Al-Azhar might suggest to many people in the West that Muslims do not regard apostasy as something problematic. This impression could be reinforced by the enshrining of the right to change one's faith within Article 18 of the United Nations' Universal Declaration of Human Rights (1948), to which many Muslim-majority countries subscribe. Surely Islam, the second largest religion in today's world with around 1.4 billion adherents, recognises this right for its own people?

In fact, however, Islam stands alone among world religions in officially prescribing a range of severe punishments for any of its adherents who choose to leave their faith, punishments that include the death sentence. As a result of this aspect of Islamic teaching, most Muslim people feel a strong hostility towards apostates, and many feel they are justified – indeed duty-bound – to harass, attack or even kill former Muslims. In some countries apostasy is officially punishable by death (although the sentence is seldom carried out), and in some others it is treated as illegal and carries lesser punishments. As Islam becomes increasingly conservative and its calls for the full implementation of shari‘a become more insistent, the danger of a more consistent and widespread enforcing of the apostasy law increases considerably.

The goal of this book is that in the future Muslims may extend the same respect to other apostates from Islam as Al-Azhar extended to President Obama in inviting him to speak there. For this to happen, all penalties for those Muslims who choose to leave their faith must be repealed, and Muslim communities must give their members the freedom to depart without fear of reprisals. Then perhaps it will indeed be possible for Islam to engage with the rest of the world in a "dialogue of reason ... to spread values of justice and good against hatred and violence".

The book examines the issue of apostasy from Islam in three main sections, which could be called "theory", "debate" and "practice". In the first section we look at Islamic teaching on apostasy, from its origins in the Islamic sources to its incorporation in various versions of shari‘a (Islamic law), which is still considered binding by observant Muslims. In the second section, we look at the debate amongst Muslims about the classical Islamic teaching on apostasy. In the third section we review the treatment of converts from Islam in the world today.

What Classical Islam Teaches about Apostasy

Introduction

Islam is a religion of law, rituals and duties. It is not merely a personal religion, but a total way of life, an all-encompassing religious, social and political system, a unique worldview, civilisation and culture. It determines not only the way that Muslims see the whole world, but also the values that they bring to it.

Islam includes a legal system of codified and detailed rules called "shari'a". Shari'a claims to be divinely given and is of paramount importance for most Muslims. It is based on the Qur'an and *hadith* (the collected sayings and deeds of Muhammad), which are seen as divinely inspired texts, as well as on the consensus of Islamic jurists (*ijma'*) and analogical reasoning (*qiyas*). For most Muslims, shari'a, as God's revealed law, is unchangeable, though there is some flexibility in matters of interpretation. Shari'a rules every aspect of a Muslim's life, including family affairs, behavioural norms, criminal justice, politics and economics.

Shari'a is usually divided into two main parts: rituals (*'ibadat*) and social relations (*mu'amallat*). The rituals include the details of ritual purity, prayer, alms, fasting, pilgrimage and sometimes *jihad*. The social relations comprise criminal law, family law (marriage, divorce, inheritance), economic law (trade and commerce, contracts) and several other topics.

Shari'a is the key to understanding Islam's attitude to those who choose to leave it. The right to religious freedom, including the right of individuals to change their religion, is taken for granted by most people in the West. All schools (*madhahib*) of Islamic law agree, however, that adult male Muslims who abandon Islam (apostates) should be killed. Therefore, although conversion from other religions to Islam is welcomed and actively encouraged, Muslims who leave Islam for any other religion must be sentenced to death (unless they repent and return to Islam).[3]

Shari'a identifies certain specific crimes that are supposedly committed against God and his rights. These crimes constitute a separate category in shari'a criminal law as they are the only ones to have divinely-mandated, obligatory, prescribed punishments (*hudud*, singular *hadd*) that cannot be altered by humans. Three of the Islamic schools of law (Hanafi, Shafi'i and Ja'fari) claim that apostasy (*irtidad*; *murtadd* = apostate; *ridda* = to apostatise) from Islam is one such crime, and that it incurs a God-prescribed penalty of death. The other schools of law (Maliki and Hanbali), though not placing apostasy in this category and giving judges greater flexibility, still decree the death penalty for apostates. Apostasy is thus viewed as a very severe crime.

The death penalty for converts from Islam has nevertheless generated much debate because references to apostasy in the Qur'an, the primary source of Islamic law, are rather ambiguous. The *hadith* (the authoritative traditions recording the sayings and deeds of Muhammad) are much clearer and are therefore the main source used to justify the death penalty for apostates.

Muhammad Iqbal Siddiqi, a popular Pakistani writer on Islam and Islamic law, represents one end of the Muslim spectrum in his book *The Penal Law of Islam*, where he claims that

> ... the sayings and doings of the Holy Prophet (peace and blessings of Allah be upon him), the decision and practice of the Caliph Abu Bakr (Allah be pleased with him), the consensus of the opinion of the Companions of the Holy Prophet (peace and blessings of Allah be upon him) and all the later Muslim jurists, and even certain verses of the Holy Qur'an all prescribe capital punishment for an apostate.[4]

In this view he is backed by many well-known traditional and contemporary scholars, including the popular 20th-century Pakistani Muslim scholar Abul A'la Mawdudi, a founding figure of Islamism in the Indian sub-continent, whose Quranic commentary is found in millions of Muslim homes.[5]

The other end of the spectrum is represented by liberal or modernist Muslim scholars who claim that apostates cannot be put to death on the grounds of their apostasy alone, but only if they are also a danger to the Islamic state. Traditionalists, however, counter that every apostate is a danger to the Islamic social order and has committed high treason. Some modernists also argue that apostates must be given forever to repent, meaning that they can never be executed.[6]

In order to present an accurate and detailed picture of how apostasy is perceived and addressed in Islam, it is important to discuss the references to apostasy in its two main sources, the Qur'an and *hadith*. These are the foundational texts from which Islamic scholars developed the shari'a law code, which is applied to varying degrees in many Muslim countries and even in the West. Muslims assert that the Qur'an, as a divine revelation, is applicable for all people at all times. The way of Muhammad (*sunna*), his sayings and deeds as recorded in the *hadith*, is the divinely ordained pattern for applying the Qur'an, and it is the model Muslims must follow when dealing with issues that arise in new circumstances in a world very different from the one into which Islam first arrived. Having considered the teaching of these texts on the theme of apostasy, we can then examine its outworking by the five principal schools of shari'a law.

The Qur'an

The Qur'an emphasises God's punishment of apostates in the next life. Apostasy is mentioned in 13 verses scattered across various chapters (*suras*). There is no clear and unambiguous mention of any punishment in this world, but it is clear that the apostate will suffer severe punishment in the next. Here are some examples:

Sura 16:106-107, 109

106. Anyone who after accepting faith in Allah utters unbelief, except under Compulsion his heart remaining firm in faith but such as open their Breast to unbelief on them is Wrath from Allah and theirs will be a Dreadful Penalty.

107. This because they love the life of this world better than the Hereafter: and Allah will not guide those who reject faith.

109. Without doubt, in the hereafter they will perish.

These verses assume that the cause of apostasy is love of this world, rather than conversion to another religion. The next verse refers simply to a rejection of Allah:

Sura 88: 23-4

23. But if any turn away and reject God

24. God will punish him with a mighty Punishment.

Yusuf 'Ali comments on this verse that:

> The Prophet of Allah is sent to teach and direct people on the way. He is not sent to force their will, or to punish them, except in so far as he may receive authority to do so. Punishment belongs to Allah alone. And Punishment is certain in the Hereafter, when true values will be restored.[7]

Therefore, according to 'Ali's interpretation of this verse, those who reject Islam are to be punished only in the next life.

Sura 3: 86-91

86. How shall God guide those who reject faith after they accepted it and bore witness that the Apostle was true and that clear signs had come unto them? But God guides not a people unjust.

87. Of such the reward is that on them (rests) the curse of God, of His angels and of all mankind.

88. In that will they dwell; nor will their penalty be lightened nor respite be their (lot).

89. Except for those that repent (even) after that and make amends: for verily God is Oft-Forgiving Most Merciful.

90. But those who reject faith after they accepted it and then go on adding to their defiance of faith never will their repentance be accepted; for they are those who have (of set purpose) gone astray.

91. As to those who reject faith and die rejecting never would be accepted from any such as much gold as the earth contains though they should offer it for ransom. For such is (in store) a penalty grievous and they will find no helpers.

According to Mawdudi, this passage refers specifically to Jewish scholars in Arabia who refused to believe the message of Muhammad. The point these verses make is that apostates face a terrible eschatological punishment, but there is no clear implication that the fate of apostates is meant to be anything other than eternal damnation.

Despite this, a majority of Muslim scholars specifically use the following verses as justification for the belief that apostates from Islam should be killed, asserting that these texts refer to apostates in general. These verses are *sura* 88:24 "God will punish him with a mighty Punishment," and 16:106, cited above:

> Anyone who after accepting faith in Allah utters unbelief except under Compulsion his heart remaining firm in faith but such as open their Breast to unbelief on them is Wrath from Allah and theirs will be a Dreadful Penalty.

A further verse used to justify punishment for apostasy in this life is *sura* 2:217:

> … and if any of you turn back from their faith and die in unbelief, their works will bear no fruit in this life and in the Hereafter; they will be Companions of the Fire and will abide therein.

Al-Khazan's commentary on the Qur'an interprets this verse as meaning that "[a]ll the deeds of the apostate become null and void in this world and the next. He must be killed. His wife must be separated from him and he has no claims on any inheritance."[8] This commentary quotes from Malik ibn Anas, Ahmad ibn Hanbal (compilers of two of the authoritative *hadith* collections) and others and has been used extensively at the influential Al-Azhar University in Cairo. Other commentaries interpreting the verse as requiring the death of the apostate include those of al-Tha'alibi and Fakhr al-Din al-Razi, although Tabari disagrees.[9] In fact, few mainstream Muslim authorities would agree with Gibb and Kramers' *Shorter Encyclopaedia of Islam* that the Qur'an mentions nothing about a death penalty for apostasy.[10] A Qur'anic passage that, according to Muhammad Iqbal Siddiqi, "states clearly how the renegades should be treated"[11] runs as follows (*sura* 9:11-12):

11. But (even so), if they repent, establish regular prayers, and practise regular charity, – they are your brethren in Faith: (thus) do We explain the Signs in detail, for those who understand.

12. But if they violate their oaths after their covenant, and taunt you for your Faith, – fight ye the chiefs of Unfaith: for their oaths are nothing to them: that thus they may be restrained.

Mawdudi too regards this passage as meaning that war must be waged against the leaders who instigate apostasy, accepting this as definite proof that the Qur'an calls for the death penalty on apostates.[12]

A final key Qur'anic passage in the argument regarding a humanly inflicted death penalty for apostasy is in *sura* 4:88-89:

88. Why should ye be divided into two parties about the Hypocrites? God hath upset them for their (evil) deeds. Would ye guide those whom God hath thrown out of the Way? For those whom God hath thrown out of the Way, never shalt thou find the Way.

89. They but wish that ye should reject the Faith, as they do, and thus be on the same footing (as they): but take not friends from their ranks until they flee in the way of God (from what is forbidden). But if they turn renegades, seize them and slay them wherever ye find them; and (in any case) take no friends or helpers from their ranks.

Zwemer states that all standard commentaries interpret this verse as an instruction to kill apostates. For example, Baidhawi's commentary says: "Whosoever turns back from his belief (*irtada*), openly or secretly, take him and kill him wheresoever ye find him, like any other infidel. Separate yourself from him altogether. Do not accept intercession in his regard."[13]

It is important here to consider the traditional understanding of the background to this passage (Q 4:88-89). It is thought to refer to a particular group of alleged Arab converts to Islam who later relapsed into paganism.[14] These individuals, known as the Hypocrites (*munafiqun*), nearly caused a disaster for the Muslim cause when they deserted at the Battle of Uhud (625 A.D.). Afterwards, the Muslims of Medina were divided as to whether the Hypocrites should be put to the sword or left alone. Eventually a middle course was decided upon as prescribed in these verses. That is, they were treated with caution, but given the opportunity to make good ("flee from what is forbidden") and to be re-admitted into the fold of Islam. The instruction to "seize them and slay them wherever ye find them" applied to those who subsequently deserted again. They were considered both enemies and deserters and were to be punished with death, "the penalty of desertion which is enforced by all nations actually at war".[15]

It is, in fact, the commentators who have extended the instruction about seizing and slaying to apply to all apostates. This extension could be considered a legitimate part of the processes called *ijma'*, *qiyas* and *ijtihad*, which were used to formulate the shari'a. *Ijma'* means "consensus"; *qiyas* means "analogy"; and *ijtihad* means "applying reason and effort in interpretation". These processes enabled Muslims to derive all the various rules for an Islamic way of life from the primary sources of Qur'an and *hadith*.

Note on "Let there be no compulsion in religion" (Q 2:256)

The Qur'anic verse "Let there be no compulsion in religion" (*sura* 2:256) is often quoted by Muslims when describing their faith to non-Muslims. Many important classical jurists and interpreters saw this verse as having been abrogated (i.e. cancelled) by later verses such as *sura* 9:5,[16] "But when the forbidden months are past, then fight and slay the pagans wherever ye find them, and seize them, beleaguer them, and lie in wait for them in every stratagem (of war)" or *sura* 9:73, "O Prophet! strive hard against the unbelievers and the Hypocrites and be firm against them." The latter is the first possible interpretation offered by Al-Qurtubi in his *tafsir* of the Qur'an. Abrogation of earlier-dated Qur'anic verses by later-dated ones is an accepted method of Islamic interpretation, where there is a contradiction in meaning between different parts of the Qur'an.

Another interpretation offered by Al-Qurtubi is that the verse means that those who submitted through the sword should not be regarded as having been compelled or forced, even though they were![17] "It is said that it means 'do not call those who have submitted through the sword compelled or forced.'"[18]

Other traditional interpreters strictly limit the application of this verse to specific incidents in the life of Muhammad for which it was revealed; they consider that it has no further implications for Muslims.

Other interpretations include the following:

1. Muslims are free to leave their own religion without expecting any punishment. (This is a minority view held by modernists and apologists who claim that later verses and *hadith* cannot be used as a justification for ignoring a fundamental and eternal Qur'anic principle.)[19]

2. Non-Muslims are not to be forced to convert to Islam.[20]

3. Muslims are not compelled to perform specific Islamic duties; they are free to neglect, if they so choose, their religious obligations. [21]

The *Hadith*

Although the Qur'an is ambiguous on the penalty for apostasy and does not appear to have any universally applicable command to kill apostates, the *hadith* are much clearer. It is also a fact of history that apostates were killed in the time of Muhammad on his orders, and immediately after his death by the first Caliph, Abu Bakr, in the *Ridda* (apostasy) Wars.

The strongest evidence Muslim jurists use to prove that apostasy is a *hadd* offence punishable by the death penalty is based on a few *hadith*,[22] the clearest one being narrated by Ikrima, from Ibn Abbas.

Bukhari, Volume 9, Book 84, Number 57

Narrated 'Ikrima: Some Zanadiqa (atheists) were brought to 'Ali and he burnt them. The news of this event, reached Ibn 'Abbas who said, "If I had been in his place, I would not have burnt them, as Allah's Apostle forbade it, saying, 'Do not punish anybody with Allah's punishment (fire).' I would have killed them according to the statement of Allah's Apostle, 'Whoever changed his [Islamic] religion, then kill him.'"

From this *hadith* (appearing in variants in several collections) it is clear that the penalty for apostasy ordained by Muhammad is death, though this should not be by burning. It is on this *hadith* that most jurists base their view that the apostate must be sentenced to death. They point out that the words "kill him" appear as a grammatical imperative in Arabic, implying an order, which must be obeyed.[23] Although Bukhari's collection of *hadith* is considered the most authoritative collection, some scholars claim that this specific *hadith* is a weak tradition (i.e. not reliable).[24] Although this is the most direct *hadith* dealing with apostasy, there are a number of others dealing indirectly with the penalty for apostasy from Islam:

Bukhari, Volume 9, Book 83, Number 17

Narrated 'Abdullah: Allah's Apostle said: "The blood of a Muslim who confesses that none has the right to be worshipped but Allah and that I am His apostle, cannot be shed except in three cases: In Qisas for murder, a married man who commits illegal sexual intercourse, and the one who reverts (separates himself) from Islam (apostate) and leaves the Muslims.

The same *hadith* also appears with slight variations in Bukhari, 9:17; 12.169; Muslim, 11, 89–90; Abu-Dawud 4; 487; Al-Tirmidhi 993; Mishkat al Masabih, 3466. Many jurists rely on this *hadith* for their claim that Muhammad prescribed the death penalty for apostasy. Some claim, however, that those who separate themselves from the community are those who fight against it, not those who simply change their religion.[25]

Another *hadith* used to justify capital punishment for apostasy deals with some people from the tribe of 'Ukal:

Bukhari, 1.234

Narrated Abu-Qilaba: Anas said, "Some people of 'Ukal or 'Uraina tribe came to Medina and its climate did not suit them. So the Prophet ordered them to go to the herd of (Milch) camels and to drink their milk and urine (as a medicine). So they went as directed and after they became healthy, they killed the shepherd of the Prophet and drove away all the camels. The news reached the Prophet early in the morning and he sent (men) in their pursuit and they were captured and brought at noon. He then ordered to cut their hands and feet (and it was done), and their eyes were branded with heated pieces of iron, they were put in 'Al-Harra' and when they asked for water, no water was given to them." Abu-Qilaba said, "Those people committed theft and murder, became infidels after embracing Islam and fought against Allah and His Apostle." (4.261)

This *hadith* is repeated several times and implies that although the punishment for theft was the amputation of their limbs, the people were then killed for rejecting Islam and becoming infidels, i.e. apostatising. However not all jurists agree with this, some claiming the death penalty was imposed for armed robbery (*hiraba*).[26]

Female apostates

There are examples in the *hadith* of Muhammad himself ordering the execution of women for apostasy.

> On the occasion of Battle of Uhud (when Muslims had to retreat), a woman became apostate. On this the Holy Prophet (peace and blessings of Allah be upon him) said: "Ask her to repent and if she does not repent, kill her."[27]

Another *hadith* says:

> A woman named Umm Ruman committed apostasy. The Holy Prophet (peace and blessings of Allah be upon him) ordered: She may be presented Islam. Then if she repents, it would be better, otherwise she should be put to death.[28]

Burial of apostates

The following *hadith* is of interest because it implies that an apostate is not entitled to a decent burial, but that in death as in life he must be humiliated:

> Bukhari, 4.814: Anas ibn Malik

> There was a Christian who embraced Islam and read surat al-Baqarah and Aal-Imran, and he used to write (the revelations) for the Prophet (peace be upon him).

> Later on he returned to Christianity again and he used to say: "Muhammad knows nothing but what I have written for him."

> Then Allah caused him to die, and the people buried him, but in the morning they saw that the earth had thrown his body out. They said, "This is the act of Muhammad and his companions. They dug the grave of our companion and took his body out of it because he had run away from them."

They again dug the grave deeply for him, but in the morning they again saw that the earth had thrown his body out. They said, "This is an act of Muhammad and his companions. They dug the grave of our companion and threw his body outside it, for he had run away from them."

They dug the grave for him as deep as they could, but in the morning they again saw that the earth had thrown his body out. So they believed that what had befallen him was not done by human beings and had to leave him thrown till vultures and dogs eat his or her body.

Reward in paradise for killers of apostates

An important factor encouraging obedience to the command to kill apostates is the special reward in paradise earned by the killer according to the *hadith*. Sahih Muslim and Bukhari record this as follows:

Bukhari, 4.808: Ali ibn Abu Talib

I relate the traditions of Allah's Messenger (peace be upon him) to you for I would rather fall from the sky than attribute something to him falsely. But when I tell you a thing which is between you and me, then no doubt, war is guile.

I heard Allah's Messenger (peace be upon him) saying, "In the last days of this world there will appear some young foolish people who will use (in their claim) the best speech of all people (i.e. the Qur'an) and they will abandon Islam as an arrow going through the game: Their belief will not go beyond their throats (i.e. they will have practically no belief), so wherever you meet them, kill them, for he who kills them shall get a reward on the Day of Resurrection."

A similar hadith is found in Sahih Muslim, 2328.

Opportunity to repent?

There are contradictory traditions concerning whether an apostate should be given a chance to repent. The story of Mu'adh who would not dismount until the apostate had been killed suggests that no opportunity to repent need be given. However, in Abu Dawud's version of this tradition, it is added that they had tried in vain to convert the apostate back to Islam.

Bukhari, 5.632: Abu Sa'id al-Khudri,

The Prophet (peace be upon him) sent Abu Musa and Mu'adh to Yemen and said to both of them "Facilitate things for the people (be kind and lenient) and do not make things difficult (for them). Give them good tidings, and do not repulse them; and both of you should obey each other."

Once Mu'adh asked Abu Musa, "How do you recite the Qur'an?" Abu Musa replied, "I recite it while I am standing, sitting or riding my riding animals, at intervals and piecemeal." Mu'adh said, "But I sleep and then get up. I sleep and hope for Allah's reward for my sleep as I seek His reward for my night prayer."

Then he (i.e. Mu'adh) pitched a tent and they started visiting each other.

Once Mu'adh paid a visit to Abu Musa and saw a chained man. Mu'adh asked, "What is this?" Abu Musa said, "(He was) a Jew who embraced Islam and has now turned apostate." Mu'adh said, "I will surely chop off his neck." And Mu'adh did it in such a way that maximum pain is caused to the chained man. Indeed he did according to the instruction the messenger of Allah had given him.

Abu Dawud, Book 38, 4341

Abu Musa said: the Prophet (peace be upon him) came to me when I was in the Yemen. A man who was Jew embraced Islam and then retreated from Islam. When the Prophet came (peace be upon him), he said: I will not come down from my mount until he is killed. He was then killed. One of them said: He was asked to repent before that.

One of the narrators said his eyes were taken out before he was killed and the Prophet (peace be upon him) liked the way he was killed.

A tradition recorded by Malik describes Caliph 'Umar's horror at the idea of executing an apostate without giving him a chance to repent:

Malik's al-Muwatta, 36:16

Did you then not shut him up for three days and give him a round loaf daily and try to induce him to repent? Perhaps he would have repented and returned to obedience to God. O God! I was not there, I did not order it and I do not approve; see, it was thus reported to me.

The Shari'a

The Islamic legal code, the shari'a, was derived from the Qur'an and *hadith* using the methodology of *ijma'*, *qiyas* and *ijtihad*. There are different schools in Islamic law, but their rulings on apostasy are all very similar, and they are unanimous in prescribing death for adult male apostates. Sunni Islam is divided into four schools of law called Hanafi, Maliki, Shafi'i and Hanbali after the four great imams who founded them. The main Shi'a school is the Ja'fari or Imami-Shi'i school. (See table on pp28–29.)

Shari'a differentiates between *hudud* and *ta'zir* offences. In a *ta'zir* offence the judge has flexibility in determining the punishment. The punishments for *hudud* crimes are found in the Qur'an, and they are therefore divinely ordained and cannot be changed by humans. They must be applied without mitigation even if the offender repents. *Hudud* punishments include 100 lashes or stoning to death for adultery, 80 lashes for false accusation of adultery, amputation of limbs for theft, 40 or 80 lashes for drinking alcohol, imprisonment, amputation or death (by crucifixion in serious cases) for highway robbery, and the death penalty for apostasy from Islam. (Though not all schools of law identify apostasy as a *hadd* offence, they all prescribe the death penalty for it.)

These shari'a punishments are the ones most offensive to modern western sensibilities, but many Islamic scholars, academics and popular preachers support the present-day application of *hudud* punishments, seeing them as identity markers of true Islamic revival. Thus, following the call by Tariq Ramadan, a popular European Muslim scholar, for a moratorium on *hudud* punishments, several Islamic scholars responded negatively. One claimed that harshness was part of shari'a and any attempt at softening it was a capitulation to western Christian concepts incompatible with Islam.

The Punishment for Apostates from Islam, According to the Five Main Schools of Shari'a

	Hanafi (Sunni)	Shafi'i (Sunni)	Maliki (Sunni)	Hanbali (Sunni)	Ja'fari (Shi'a)
Sane Adult Male	Death	Death	Death	Death	Death
Sane Adult Female	Imprisoned until she repents	Death	Death	Death	Imprisoned and beaten with rods until she repents or dies
Child	Imprisoned; killed only on reaching maturity	Imprisoned; killed only on reaching maturity and if a voluntary convert to Islam	Killed only on reaching maturity	Killed only on reaching maturity and if a voluntary convert to Islam	Killed only on reaching maturity
Period for Repentance	Three days	Three days	Three days	Immediate repentance may be required	Born Muslims must repent immediately; converts to Islam are given time to repent

Apostasy a *hadd* offence	Yes	Yes	No	No	Yes
Must apostasy be spoken to incur penalty?	Yes	No – inward apostasy is punishable	No – inward apostasy is punishable	No – inward apostasy is punishable	No – inward apostasy is punishable
Establishing Guilt	Two witnesses required	Even words spoken in jest are counted as apostasy; two witnesses required	Ascertain whether the individual was previously a true practising Muslim		Confession and two truthful male witnesses; words spoken in anger, jest, and unintentionally do not count.
Other Features	Desirable to explain the Islamic faith to the apostate, in hope that he or she will repent		Emphasis on three-day period for repentance		

A summary of Sunni laws on apostasy is given in Mohammed Al-Abdari Ibn-Hadj's famous book *Al Madkhal*. All schools agree that it is permitted to kill apostates from in front or from behind, that their shed blood requires no vengeance, that their property belongs to true believers, and finally that their marriage ties become null and void.[29]

All schools of law state that only the ruler or his deputy can carry out the execution of the apostate. At the same time, however, they claim that the apostate's life is forfeit and of no value, and if a private individual kills him, the killer is not to be punished in any way, nor has he to pay blood money. The door is thus opened for anyone to take the law into his or her own hands and kill the apostate.[30]

1. The Hanafi School[31]

The Hanafi school of law is dominant in Turkey and the Indian sub-continent. Many rules on apostasy and its legal consequences are found in the *Hedaya*, a famous and authoritative textbook of Hanafi law.

Definition of apostasy: Apostasy is categorised under the *hudud* offences.

Punishment for apostasy: The *Hedaya* categorically states that there are only two options for an apostate: Islam or death. "There are only two modes of repelling the sin of apostasy, namely, *destruction* or *Islam*."[32]

Attempt at gaining the apostate's repentance: The *Hedaya* lays down the following procedure for dealing with apostasy: The Islamic faith may be explained to the apostate, in the hope that he may be persuaded and reassured of the rightness of Islam. This step is not obligatory, but it is desirable and strongly encouraged.[33] The apostate is to be imprisoned for three days, and if he has not returned to the faith by the end of that time, he is then to be killed. Various arguments for and against the three-day waiting rule are given.[34]

Minors who apostasise: A boy who is a minor is not killed but imprisoned.[35] The Hanafis regard the Islam of a minor as valid, but in Islamic law he is held to be incapable of an act that might injure himself, and they apply this rule by disregarding his apostasy. Only if a minor is an apostate on reaching maturity is he to be killed.[36]

Children and grandchildren of apostates: The *Hedaya* also contains complex rules about the status of children and grandchildren of apostates. In general, the children are also regarded as apostates and may in some circumstances be "compelled" to become Muslims, whereas an apostate's grandchild is considered "an original infidel and an enemy".[37] The descendents of an apostate who has left to reside in a foreign country are the property of the Muslim state, should the foreign country be conquered by the Muslims.[38] If an apostate's children become apostates or if he has children during his apostasy, they cannot inherit from him.[39]

Female apostates: Female apostates are not to be killed but imprisoned until they return to Islam.[40]

The punishment of someone who kills an apostate before he had a chance to repent: No penalty is incurred by anyone who kills an apostate before he has been given an exposition of the faith, even though such a premature killing is "abominable".[41]

Mentally ill and drunk: The mentally ill and those intoxicated by alcohol are not held responsible for their action.[42]

Marriage: A man's apostasy requires an immediate separation from his wife, since Muslim women are not permitted to marry non-Muslim men.[43] The Muslim wife of an apostate inherits from him.[44]

Property and estate of an apostate: An apostate loses his right to his property until he returns to Islam.[45] If a person dies (or is killed) in his apostasy, the property that he acquired before his apostasy is given to his Muslim heirs. Property that was acquired during his apostasy goes to the public treasury.[46] A female apostate's estate goes in its entirety to her heirs.[47]

The purchase, sale, manumission, mortgage or gift of an apostate's property are suspended. If he returns to Islam they are valid, but if he dies, is killed or flees to another country the acts are null.[48]

If an apostate defector returns to Muslim territory and has again become Muslim, he may regain from his heirs any of his territory that they hold.[49] A Muslim man cannot inherit from his apostate wife unless she apostatised during sickness.[50]

2. The Maliki School[51]

The Maliki school of law is predominant in North and West Africa.

Definition of apostasy: Apostasy is categorised as a *ta'zir* offence.Punishment for apostasy: A Maliki manual on shari'a by al-Qayrawani (922-996), *Al-Risala*, has this to say on apostasy and similar "crimes":

37.19 CRIMES AGAINST ISLAM

A freethinker (*zindiq*) must be put to death and his repentance is rejected. A freethinker is one who conceals his unbelief and pretends to follow Islam. A magician also is to be put to death, and his repentance also is to be rejected. An apostate is also killed unless he repents. He is allowed three days grace; if he fails to utilise the chance to repent, the execution takes place. This same also applies to women apostates.

If a person who is not an apostate admits that prayer is obligatory but will not perform it, then such a person is given an opportunity to recant by the time of the next prayer; if he does not utilise the opportunity to repent and resume worship, he is then executed. If a Muslim refuses to perform the pilgrimage, he should be left alone and God himself shall decide this case. If a Muslim should abandon the performance of prayer because he disputes its being obligatory, then such a person shall be treated as an apostate – he should be given three days within which to repent. If the three days lapse without his repenting, he is then executed.

Whoever abuses the Messenger of God – peace and blessing of God be upon him – is to be executed, and his repentance is not accepted.

Attempt at gaining the apostate's repentance: The apostate should be confined for three days and given the chance to repent; a judgment requiring the apostate to be killed before the end of the three days is valid, however. If the apostate does not repent then he is killed; his body is neither washed nor buried. In line with *sura* 4:137, the repentance of the apostate is not accepted in the case of a repeat offence.

Female apostates: According to this school, women as well as men should be put to death for apostasy. A female apostate is killed if she does not repent in three days. A woman who is pregnant, nursing a child, or divorced and in the waiting period when she can still return to her husband will have her death sentence postponed.

Mentally ill and drunks: The apostasy of a drunken person is valid.

Heretics: A heretic (a Muslim who holds beliefs regarded as deviant by the orthodox majority) or hypocrite (someone who pretends to be a good Muslim but does not really believe in his/her heart) is not given the chance to repent but is killed immediately.[52]

Marriage of an apostate: The marriage of an apostate is dissolved without any need for a divorce procedure.

Property of an apostate: The property of an apostate after his execution is regarded as spoils of war to be shared by the Muslim community.

Treatment of apostates who have not been killed: Like the Hanafi School, the Maliki School lays down detailed rules about the treatment of apostates who have avoided execution. These include the following (which assume that the apostate has embraced Christianity): Muslims are forbidden to give branches to an apostate to carry on Palm Sunday, to sell him wood from which a crucifix might be made or copper from which bells could be cast, or to transfer a house in order that it may be used as a church. In addition, Muslims are forbidden to buy an animal slaughtered by an apostate, or to lend or hire to an apostate either their slave or an animal to ride.[53]

3. The Shafi'i School

The Shafi'i school is predominant in Indonesia, Malaysia and the Philippines.

Definition of apostasy: Shafi'is view apostasy as a *hadd* offence. Shafi'i teaching given by Nawawi in his book *Minhaj-at-Talibin*, which is a standard work in Egypt, South India, Malaysia and Indonesia, defines apostasy as follows:

> Apostasy consists in the abjuration of Islam, either mentally, or by words, or by acts incompatible with faith. As to oral abjuration, it matters little whether the words are said in joke, or through a spirit of contradiction, or in good faith. But before such words can be considered as a sign of apostasy they must contain a precise declaration:
>
> 1. That one does not believe in the existence of the Creator, or of His apostles; or

2. That Mohammed, or one of the other apostles, is an impostor; or

3. That one considers lawful what is strictly forbidden by the ijma e.g. the crime of fornication; or

4. That one considers to be forbidden what is lawful according to the ijma; or

5. That one is not obliged to follow the precepts of the ijma, as well positive as negative; or

6. That one intends shortly to change one's religion; or that one has doubts upon the subject of the truth of Islam, etc.

As to acts, these are not considered to be incompatible with faith, unless they show a clear indication of a mockery or denial of religion, as e.g. throwing the Koran upon a muck heap or prostrating oneself before an idol, or worshipping the sun.[54]

Punishment for apostasy: The death of all adult apostates, regardless of gender, is required.[55] The classical Shafi'i manual of law, *'Umdat al-Salik (The Reliance of the Traveller)* by Ahmad ibn Naqib al-Misri (d. 1368), states the principle that a sane adult Muslim who apostatises must be killed if he or she does not repent.[56]

o8.0 APOSTASY FROM ISLAM (RIDDA)

o8.0 Leaving Islam is the ugliest form of unbelief (kufr) and the worst...

o8.1 When a person who has reached puberty and is sane voluntarily apostatises from Islam, he deserves to be killed.

o8.2 In such a case, it is obligatory for the caliph to ask him to repent and return to Islam. If he does, it is accepted from him, but if he refuses, he is immediately killed.

[Note: 'o' denotes an excerpt from the commentary of Sheikh 'Umar Barakat.]

Attempt at gaining the apostate's repentance: Anwar Ahmad Qadri, a Pakistani lawyer, in his book *A Sunni Shafi'i Law Code*, which is a translation of *Mukhtasar fil Risalah* by a classical Shafi'i jurist, Abu Shuja' al-Isfahani (d. 1106), states:[57]

Art. 113 *Rules for Apostates.* It is obligatory to ask the person apostatising from the religion of Islam, or on *irtidad,* 1 to offer *taubah* [repentance] three times; then it is good if he did it, otherwise, he shall be killed 2; then, he will neither be given a bath, nor any funeral prayer, and so also, he will not be buried in the graveyard of Muslims.

1. May be a male or a female, as he or she refuses to accept Allah, or falsifies any of the Prophets or holds as legal the things held *haram* [forbidden] by consensus or *ijma'.*

2. If a free man, the imam will kill him but not by burning; if anyone kills him except the imam, he will be punished by *ta'zir* [not by *hudud*; the judge has discretion in deciding on the punishment]; if the apostate is a slave, the master will kill him.

Minors who apostasise: Nawawi states that minors are not responsible for their apostasy. Minors are thought to follow their parents in religion, so a minor who is forced to accept Islam by his parents is not to be killed even on reaching maturity, as his Islam is not regarded as "original" to him and is therefore not valid. But if he accepts Islam in full faith (that is, voluntarily) and then apostatises, he must be killed on reaching maturity.

Children and grandchildren of apostates: On the status of the children of apostates, Nawawi writes:

> The child of an apostate remains a Moslem, without regard to the time of its conception, or to one of its parents remaining a Moslem or not. One authority, however, considers the child whose father and mother have abjured the faith to be an apostate, while another considers such a child to be by origin an infidel. (The child should be considered as an apostate. This is what the jurists of Iraq have handed down to us as the universally accepted theory.)

Female apostates: The apostate woman must repent within three days or face the death penalty.

The punishment of someone who kills an apostate before he had a chance to repent: According to 'Umdat al-Salik:

o8.4 There is no indemnity for killing an apostate (O: or any expiation, since it is killing someone who deserves to die).

Mentally ill and drunk: The mentally ill are not responsible for their apostasy. Drunkenness, however, is not considered an excuse for apostasy in the Shafi'i school.

Property and estate of an apostate: on the subject of an apostate's property Nawawi states:

> As to the ownership of the property of an apostate dead in impenitence, it remains in suspense, i.e. the law considers it as lost from the moment of abjuration of the faith; but in case of repentance it is considered never to have been lost. However, there are several other theories upon the subject, though all authorities agree that debts contracted before apostasy, as well as the personal maintenance of the apostate during the period of exhortation, are charges upon the estate. It is the same with any damages due in consequence of pecuniary prejudice caused to other persons, the maintenance of his wives, whose marriage remains in suspense, and the maintenance of his descendant or descendants. Where it is admitted that ownership remains in suspense, the same principle must be applied to dispositions subsequent to apostasy, in so far as they are capable of being suspended, such as an enfranchisement by will, and legacies, which all remain intact where the exhortation is successful, though not otherwise. On the other hand, dispositions which, by their very nature, do not admit of such suspension, such as sale, pledging, gift, and enfranchisement by contract, are null and void ab initio, though Shafi'i, in his first period, wished to leave them in suspense. All authorities, however, are agreed that an apostate's property may in no case be left at his disposition, but must be deposited in charge of some person of irreproachable character. But a female slave may not be so entrusted to a man; she must be entrusted to some trustworthy woman. An apostate's property must be leased out, and it is to the court that the slave undergoing enfranchisement by contract should make his periodical payments.[58]

Apostasy under compulsion: Apostasy under violent compulsion is overlooked.

4. The Hanbali School

The Hanbali School of law is predominant in Saudi Arabia and Qatar.

Definition of apostasy: The Hanbali school sees apostasy as a *ta'zir* offence.

Attempt at gaining the apostate's repentance: There are two opinions: some state that the apostate should be given a period of three days for repentance; others that he should be offered Islam and if he refuses he is to be immediately killed.[59]

Repeat apostate: According to Ibn Hanbal, the repentance of the believer who apostatises is not accepted if repeated, based on *sura* 4, verse 137:

> Those who believe, and then disbelieve, and then believe, and then disbelieve, and then increase in unbelief – Allah is not likely to forgive them nor to guide them on any way.

Minors who apostasise: If a boy who became a Muslim with his parents is an apostate by the time he reaches maturity, he is not then killed, since his faith in Islam began when he was dependent on others. Rather he is to be forced to return to Islam by being arrested and beaten. If however a boy comes to Islam on his own but is an apostate when he reaches maturity, he must then be killed.

Children and grandchildren of apostates: Hanbalites permit the descendents and descendents' descendents of apostates to be enslaved.

Female apostates: Women are treated in the same way as men; they must be killed if they do not repent immediately.

The punishment of someone who kills an apostate before he had a chance to repent: If an apostate is killed prior to his being called to repentance, the killer is not punished or required to pay blood money.

Mentally ill and drunk: The apostasy of a drunkard is overlooked, it is not valid. The apostasy of a drunken person is valid.

Heretics: Heretics are killed without being given the opportunity to repent.

Property and estate of an apostate: The ownership of the property is suspended until the apostate is executed. Then it becomes the properly of the Muslim community and is transferred to the public purse.

Shi'a law

Shi'a Islam remained in close contact with Sunni Islam during the development of the four Sunni schools of law. Consequently, Shi'a law closely resembles Sunni law, differing from it no more than the four schools differ from each other.[60]

Definition of apostasy: Apostasy is categorised as one of the *hudud* offences.

Punishment for apostasy:

> Every individual of the male sex who, born in the religion of Islam, apostasizes, no longer enjoys the protection of Islam, but is ipso facto condemned to death. His wife should be separated from him; and his property is confiscate.[61]

Children and grandchildren of apostates: A child born of a heretic after the apostasy of the father, and of a Muslim mother, and conceived after the apostasy, is subject to the same conditions as his parents; and if he is assassinated, the murderer cannot be punished by the law of retaliation.[62]

Female apostates: The woman guilty of apostasy is not punished with death, even if she was born in the Muslim faith, but she is condemned to perpetual imprisonment, and is to be beaten with rods at the hours of prayer.[63]

Methods of carrying out the death penalty for apostasy and blasphemy

The methods of executing those sentenced to death for apostasy or blasphemy have always been brutal and cruel. Decapitation and crucifixion were popular, but burning was practised too. The idea was not just to implement the law, but also to make the process as humiliating as possible. Ibn Warraq lists some of the methods used in Islamic history:

> In general, execution must be by the sword, though there are examples of apostates tortured to death, or strangled, burnt, drowned, impaled or flayed. The caliph Umar used to tie them to a post and had lances thrust into their hearts.[64]

Here are a few examples offered by Qadi 'Iyad:

> The fuqaha' of the Qayrawan and the companions of Sahnun

gave a fatwa for the killing of Ibrahim al-Ghazari, a poet and master of many sciences. He was one of those who attended the assembly of Qadi Abu'l-'Abbas ibn Talib for debate. He was accused of objectionable things like mocking Allah, His Prophets and our Prophet. Qadi Yahya ibn 'Umar and the other fuqaha' summoned him and commanded that he be killed and crucified. He was stabbed and crucified upside down. Then he was brought down and burned.[65]

Abu'l Mus'ab said: "A Christian was brought to me who said, 'By the One who chose 'Isa over Muhammad'. There was a dispute about him before me. So I beat him until I killed him, or he lived a day and a night. I commanded someone to drag him by the feet and throw him onto a dungheap and the dogs ate him".[66]

Ibn Kinana said in Al-Mabsut that any Jew or Christian who reviles the Prophet can be burned by the Imam. If he likes, he can kill him and then burn his body. If he likes, he can burn him alive when he is so bold as to curse him.[67]

Muslims Debate and Interpret the Apostasy Law

Scholars discuss the death sentence

Having examined apostasy in the context of the Islamic sources, it is important also to relate it to the Islamic social context. In view of the scarcity and ambiguity of Qur'anic references to any humanly imposed penalty for apostasy, how did the requirement of capital punishment for apostasy arise? Muslim apologists often say that it was largely generated by the activities of some Jewish and Muslim "hypocrites" in the very early years of Islam[68] who conspired to create confusion in the newly formed Muslim community by professing to convert to Islam and then renouncing it. This alleged conspiracy, of which the goals were supposed to be entirely political, was countered ruthlessly by Muhammad, who ordered those responsible for the treachery to be killed.

Soon after Muhammad's death, a similar situation arose in the form of the *Ridda* (apostasy) wars of rebellion against Caliph Abu Bakr, Muhammad's successor as leader of the Islamic state. Both were attacks upon the political authority of the Muslim ruler, as opposed to simple conversion to another faith.

It seems, therefore, that in spite of the Qur'anic statement forbidding "compulsion in religion" (2:256), many later Muslim writers did not take account of the contexts in which punishments were implemented. They fastened on apostasy as the action to be punished rather than on the political conspiracy that was the alleged reason for the apostasy. Zwemer held that early Islamic law and practice regarding apostasy were probably less rigid and less severe than those that were codified after Islam had spread beyond Arabia. He asserts that many of the *hadith* regarding apostates were created to claim divine authority and Muhammad's example for policies that originated later.[69] Indeed, the contemporary Lebanese scholar, Subhi Mahmassani, claims that Muhammad never killed anyone merely for apostasy; rather the death penalty was imposed only when apostasy was linked to an act of political betrayal of the Muslim community.[70]

The late Zaki Badawi, president of the Muslim College in London, argued that the death penalty for apostasy was formulated under the Umayyads (661-750) and the 'Abbasids (750-1254) and then became normative doctrine in all the schools of Islamic law. He stated, "[E]arlier jurists, with a few exceptions, supported the death penalty for the apostate and this remains the case to the present day."[71]

But Badawi also noted that a minority of scholars, such as Ibrahim al-Nakhi (d. 713), opposed the death penalty, arguing that the apostate should be given unlimited time to recant. Al-Nakhi could find no evidence in the Qur'an for capital punishment, and he did not accept the *hadith* calling for the death sentence as authentic. (He too accepted the principle of coercion, however, which called for the apostate to be induced to recant.) But al-Nakhi's opinion was ignored by the founders of the law schools.[72]

El-'Awa, an Egyptian lawyer and Islamic scholar, believes that as the Qur'an itself does not prescribe a punishment for apostasy this should fall into the *ta'zir* (discretionary) rather than *hadd* (compulsory) category. It would then be possible to distinguish between simple changes of religion, for which no punishment needs to be applied, and cases in which harm is caused to society, for which punishment must be inflicted. He claims that there have always been a small minority of jurists holding to this position, including the famous medieval scholar Ibn-Taymiyya.[73]

The view that prevailed, however, was that the death penalty should be inflicted for apostasy. Because Islam is seen as a total way of life with no separation of religion from politics and the state, and because Islam is seen as the basis of the legitimate state and its legal system, desertion from Islam was treated as political treason. The result of this merging of political and religious issues is that in Muslim-majority countries conversion from Islam to another religion is still viewed as a treasonable and shameful defection. During times of war, many states punish defection with death, and as Islam traditionally considers itself to be in a perpetual battle with *kufr* (unbelief), apostasy can be seen as betrayal and treason. Dr Y. Zaki, a leading British convert to Islam, emphasised this viewpoint in a discussion on BBC radio in 1991: "Islam is not just a religion; it's a state, and Islam does not distinguish between sacred and secular authority ... apostasy and treason are one and the same thing." Since treason is punishable by death, he argued, so too is apostasy.[74]

Abul A'la Mawdudi took a similar position, arguing that Islam is not simply a religion like Christianity, but a complete order of life embracing all spheres and serving as the basis of society, state and civilisation. As such it cannot allow itself to be made "the toy of individual free wills". Fundamental differences, he says, cannot be accepted in such a system (though minor differences are), and an apostate who has demonstrated that he is not willing to assimilate into his society's order must be cast out of it, for he has rejected its very foundation. Mawdudi states that it is preferable for an apostate to emigrate from a Muslim state, but if he stays he becomes a great danger to society, spreading a malignant plague among the population that must be eliminated by the death penalty.[75]

Abdurahman Abdulkadir Kurdi, professor of Qur'an and *Sunna* at Umm al-Qura University, Mecca, Saudi Arabia, makes the same point, stating that:

> The law of apostasy is equal to the man-made law of treason, with one important distinction; it is not tantamount to denouncing or breaking with one's country. Renouncing Islam is regarded as a betrayal of faith in God Himself and a denunciation of kinship. Capital punishment is the penalty in man-made law for treasonable action and has become recognized internationally as the norm or standard law for such a crime.

Seeking to emphasize the merciful nature of Islam he goes on to say:

> Repentance is required before executing the penalty. Sentence must be delayed for at least three days if there is hope of repentance, even though the penitent is not sincere. Will any sort of man-made law accept such repentance in a case of treason? No such understanding of human weakness has been exhibited among the community of nations yet.[76]

Muhammad Iqbal Siddiqi, attempting to counter the argument that the Islamic punishment for apostasy is too severe, writes:

If Islam were a mere religion in the sense in which this term is commonly used, a hotchpotch of dogmas and rituals, having no direct relation with the economic, political and social structure of society, then such severe punishment for apostasy would have certainly been the height of high-handedness because the change of religion would not have, in the least, disturbed the social order. But the problem is that in Islam the Kingdom of Heaven whose foundations are firstly laid in the heart of man is to be essentially externalised in every phase of social set up i.e. in politics, in economics, in law, in manners and in international relations. In such circumstances it is quite obvious that when a person rebels against the Kingdom of Heaven within his heart, he commits high treason against the Kingdom of Heaven on earth, the visible and concrete expression of the Kingdom of Heaven within the heart. The persons who commit treason are always dealt with severely in every political order. A stern attitude is always adopted by all sane governments against rebels and disruptionists, and so is the case with Islam. There is nothing unusual in what Islam has done. In Islam religion is not a matter of private relationship between man and Allah, but is intertwined with society. So when he abandons Islam he in fact revolts against the authority of the Islamic State and society."[77]

Al-Azhar University is of the opinion that apostasy is a *hadd* crime. In extracts from the proceedings of Al-Azhar's Fourth Conference of the Academy of Islamic Research (1968) the following passage on the death penalty for an apostate (*murtadd*) appears:[78]

A murtadd is one who turns back from Islam to disbelief and error. Never could a man who has tasted the sweetness of Islam think of relapsing into unbelief.

The punishment for apostasy is instituted in the following traditions:

(a) Whoever changes his religion, put him to death.

(b) It is unlawful to shed a Muslim's blood excepting only for one of three causes, namely, adultery after marriage, life for life and apostasy.

(c) It is related that Muadh Ibn Djabal came to Abu Musa al-Ashari at whom he found tied man (*sic*). On hearing that this man was a

Jew, then became a Muslim, then returned back to his first religion, Muadh refused to sit down until the apostate had been slain, saying three times, Such is the decision of Allah and of his Apostle.

(d) It is related that the Prophet, on hearing that a woman called Umm Marwan had apostatised from Islam, directed that she should be asked to repent, otherwise she would be killed.

Yusuf al-Qaradawi, the popular Qatari cleric often described as moderate by Western media and politicians, states that the majority view of Muslim jurists supports the death penalty for apostasy:

> All Muslim jurists agree that the apostate is to be punished. However, they differ regarding the punishment itself. The majority of them go for killing; meaning that an apostate is to be sentenced to death.[79]

Al-Qaradawi also lists other implications of a Muslim's being defined as an apostate:

> Accusing a Muslim of *kufr* is a very serious matter which entails very serious consequences – his killing and the confiscation of his property become lawful. As a *kafir*, he must be separated from his wife and children; there can be no bond between him and other Muslims; he must be deprived of his inheritance and cannot be inherited from; he must be denied the Islamic burial and the *salah* for the dead person; and he must not be buried in a Muslim graveyard.[80]

(For a fuller statement of al-Qaradawi's views on apostasy, see Appendix 1 on pp101–118.)

When modernisation first impacted the Muslim world following the progress of Western colonialism and its imposition of secular laws and education systems, the old tensions between the interpretations of Muslim conservatives and Muslim liberals rose to the surface again. Liberal reformers tried to reconcile Islam with modernity using the flexible principles of reason and the public good to reinterpret shari'a along modern lines. Some contemporary liberals argue that shari'a laws are human interpretations of the eternally fixed principles of Islam, so they can be changed to fit modern contexts; it is only the basic principles that are immutable.

The majority of Muslims, however, and especially Islamists (Islamic fundamentalists) still see shari'a as divinely inspired and completely unchangeable, valid for all times and places. Therefore they reject the liberal arguments.

Links to blasphemy and heresy

In Islamic jurisprudence and tradition, apostasy has always been linked to blasphemy and heresy. These three concepts are sub-categories of a main category known as *kufr* (unbelief). So although the terms are distinct in English, they are closely linked in the minds of Muslims and are sometimes used interchangeably. As Abdullah and Hassan Saeed explain:

> I have noted the diversity of views on apostasy and how a person comes to be regarded as an apostate. These views appear to combine – and even collapse – the concepts of apostasy, hypocrisy, heresy and unbelief into apostasy ... A Muslim may be accused of apostasy, blasphemy, hypocrisy, heresy or unbelief on the basis of the same action or utterance. Different Muslims may use different terms to express what such an action or utterance entails. In cases where a Muslim is accused of one of these offences, the punishment, generally speaking, is death as specified in pre-modern Islamic legal texts.[81]

We have seen already that there is a unanimous consensus among the schools of Islamic law that apostasy is punishable by death, and that some regard it as a *hadd* crime for which the penalty is fixed by God. Blasphemy and heresy are also regarded as severe crimes, and in some cases they carry the same penalty. Blasphemy is legally a *ta'zir* offence, for which the judge has flexibility in determining the punishment, not a *hadd* crime.[82] But because of the close connection between blasphemy and apostasy the penalty is the same. For the same reason the various offences are often combined in single prosecutions.[83]

Blasphemy is mainly defined as the cursing, reviling or insulting of Muhammad (and/or other prophets), a serious offence that incurs the death penalty. God has highly exalted Muhammad above any other human being and reviling him has been expressly forbidden by God.[84] An often-quoted, obscure *hadith* says:

'Ali b Abi Talib reported from the Prophet, who said: Anyone who reviles [curses] me, kill him immediately.[85]

For example, according to the Maliki school of shari'a, insulting Muhammad or any of the prophets of Islam is punishable by death, and repentance is not to be accepted (although if Allah is insulted repentance is to be accepted).[86]

Likewise the Shafi'i school rules that someone who slanders Muhammad or insults one of the prophets of Islam is to be killed without being given the opportunity to repent. Abu Bakr al-Farsi al-Shafi'i said, "It is unanimously agreed among the companions of the Prophet and their companions that the punishment for reviling the Prophet is death. The death sentence must be carried out immediately and must not be delayed for any reason whatsoever."[87]

Abu Hanifa, founder of the Hanafi school of law, is reported to have said, "Any person who reviles or insults the Prophet of Allah or abuses him or attributes lies to him will be considered an apostate whose blood should be shed."[88]

A similar quote is attributed also to Ahmad Ibn Hanbal, founder of the Hanbali school of law: "any person who reviles the Prophet and abuses him or his family, whether he be a Muslim or a non-Muslim, should be condemned to death and executed. His apology cannot be accepted."[89]

The verdict of shari'a is set out clearly in the authoritative and influential book *Ash Shifa* by the 12th century Maliki jurist Qadi 'Iyad (1083-1149):

The Judgement of the Shari'a regarding someone who curses or disparage the Prophet[90]

Know that all who curse Muhammad, may Allah bless him and grant him peace, or blame him or attribute imperfection to him in his person, lineage, his deen or any of his qualities, or alludes to that or its like by any means whatsoever, whether in the form of a curse or contempt or belittling him or detracting from him or finding fault with him or maligning him, the judgement regarding such a person is the same as the judgement against anyone who curses him. He is killed as we shall make clear. This judgement extends to anything which amounts to a curse or disparagement.

We have no hesitation concerning this matter, be it a clear statement or allusion.

The same applies to anyone who curses him, invokes against him, desires to harm him, ascribes to him what does not befit his position or jokes about his mighty affair with foolish talk, satire, dislikes words [sic] or lies, or reviles him because of any affliction or trial which happened to him or disparages him, because of any of the permissible and well-known human events which happened to him. All of this is the consensus of the 'ulama' and the imams of *fatwa* from the time of the Companions until today.

Abu Bakr al-Mundhir said that the bulk of the people of knowledge agree that whoever curses the Prophet is killed. These include Malik ibn Anas, al-Layth, Ahmad ibn Hanbal and Ishaq ibn Rahawayh, and it is the position of the Shafi'i school.

...

In the Mabsut from 'Uthman ibn Kinana we find, "Any Muslim who reviles the Prophet is killed or crucified without being asked to repent. The imam can choose between crucifying him or killing him". In the variant of Abu'l Mus'ab and Ibn Abi Uways, they heard Malik say, "Anyone who curses the Messenger of Allah, may Allah bless him and grant him peace, reviles him, finds fault with him or disparages him is killed, be he Muslim or unbeliever, without being asked to repent."[91]

...

Ibn Wahb related that Malik said, "Anyone who says that the Prophet's cloak (or button) is dirty, thereby intending to find fault with him, should be killed.[92]

There is no argument between scholars as to the killing of the offender, only about whether the offence is a *hadd* or a *ta'zir* one, whether the offender should be regarded as an unbeliever or an apostate, and whether he should be granted the opportunity to repent or be killed immediately.[93]

Some authorities list 300 different acts that could be counted as *kufr*, thus providing plenty of possible reasons for denouncing other Muslims as infidels liable to the death penalty. This process is known as *takfir*.[94]

Thus in Pakistan, for example, there is no law against apostasy, but the "blasphemy law" introduced in the 1980s includes serious punishments for desecrating the Qur'an and defiling the name of Muhammad. It has been used extensively to denounce both Muslims and non-Muslims. (See below, pp65–67.)

Zaki Badawi has argued that in the early Islamic state the category of apostasy was manipulated by the rulers and the Islamic scholars of the establishment for political aims. The jurists gave apostasy a very wide definition:

> The renunciation of Islam either through converting to another religion, or becoming an atheist, or rejecting well known parts of the Shariah such as the prohibition on the consumption of wine or treating Islamic texts with disrespect, or insulting God or the Prophet or any of the Prophets mentioned in the Qur'an, or holding an unacceptable doctrine.[95]

This enabled rulers to suppress opposition by using *takfir* to label opposition leaders as apostates.

El-'Awa claims that although for other kinds of shari'a offences Muslim jurists have tried to moderate the punishment meted out to offenders, for apostasy they have made it more severe, increasing the number of cases in which the death penalty is to be implemented by broadening the words and acts that are considered to be apostasy beyond the original meaning of the word, which is simply "to change one's religion".[96] He attributes this change to the fear that apostates would serve as examples for others to follow, thus harming the public interest and weakening Islam, and also because of the strength of the Arabic imperative "kill him" in the *hadith* quoted on p22, which led the jurists to place the punishment for apostasy in the *hadd* category.[97]

Until modern times, even taking into account the historical range of views within Islam on questions of theology and law, a broad range of belief was generally tolerated and accepted. Now, however, it is not only those who have professed another faith who may be killed for "apostasy". In recent decades, as Islamists have gained in strength, they have increasingly widened the definition of an apostate to include anyone who disagrees with what they consider to be orthodox Islam. They have also moved the arguments from the sphere of literary and media polemics to that of violence and legal prosecutions.

Impact of the concept of the individual in Islam

Ali A. Allawi, a former Iraqi Minister of Defence, in his recent book *The Crisis of Islamic Civilization*,[98] discusses the concept of the individual in Islam. He argues that one of the main and deep differences between Islam and the Judeo-Christian West is a radically different view of the individual.[99] In classical Islam only God possesses real, autonomous individuality. The concept of the human individual as an autonomous entity endowed with free will simply does not exist. The individual acquires choice and will from God only at the point of performing a specific action. They are essential attributes of God and therefore cannot be innate, natural, autonomous endowments of humans.

A central premise of Islamic human rights is that the interests of Islam and the Muslim community as a whole are paramount. If there is a conflict between these and the interests of the individual, then it is the individual's freedom that must be sacrificed. This is completely at odds with the assumption of international human rights law that the individual is the best judge of his or her interests and should therefore have freedom to choose.[100]

On this view there is no room within Islam for the Western concept of the autonomous individual. The concept of the absolutely transcendent God leaves no space for the individual as a free moral being. Islam thus dissolves the individual into a totalitarian Islamic community governed by God and his revealed law (shari'a).[101] By its very nature Islam cannot therefore allow free choice, and the apostate must therefore be destroyed to preserve the integrity of its ideology. Allawi sees the Universal Declaration of Human Rights (UDHR) as a Western construct; the authors deliberately affirmed the freedom of the individual both to choose his or her faith and to change it, knowing this would always be problematical for Muslims.[102]

In 1990 Muslim leaders in Cairo produced an alternative Islamic "Cairo Declaration on Human Rights", which was adopted by all states of the Organization of the Islamic Conference (OIC). This declaration firmly subjected all human rights to the authority of shari'a,[103] thus severely limiting their scope and effectively denying the right of an individual Muslim to convert to another religion.

Amending the apostasy law?

For most contemporary Muslims across the spectrum of beliefs and ideologies, apostasy still carries shocking and dreadful associations as a most abhorrent sin. Even for modernists and secularists it can carry negative connotations of betrayal of one's community and rejection of one's heritage. This attitude explains why so few Muslim voices are ever raised in defence of those accused of apostasy. But there have been Muslim calls for a reform of the harsh apostasy law and for Islamic leaders to proclaim that it is permissible for Muslims to choose other faiths, just as non-Muslims are allowed to choose Islam.

Some modernist Islamic scholars argue from the Qur'an and from the historical context of the *hadith* that an apostate should not be put to death unless he (or she) is also a danger to the Islamic state. Thus they differ from the traditionalists in asserting the possibility of apostasy without rebellion. The definition of "danger to the Islamic state" is important, however. Sheikh Tantawi, the Grand Imam of Al-Azhar, says that an apostate "should be left alone as long as he does not pose a threat or belittle Islam". It is hard to imagine how those who have left Islam could say anything about their conversion without in some sense being critical of Islam. Muslims would then, by Tantawi's logic, be "forced to take action".

In July 2007, the Egyptian Grand Mufti, Ali Gomaa, stated in an interview on a Forum operated by *The Washington Post* and *Newsweek* that Muslims should not be punished for converting from Islam as long as they did not undermine the foundations of society. Muslims were free to change their religion, which was a matter between an individual and God; those who commit the sin of apostasy should not receive a punishment in this world, but will be punished by God on Judgement Day. Following a furore in the Egyptian media, Ali Gomaa denied he had made any such statement. *Dar al-Iftaa*, Egypt's highest body for delivering shari'a verdicts on Islam, alleged that he had in fact said that "Islam forbids Muslims from renouncing their faith ... if a Muslim did they would be committing a mortal sin ...

apostasy is a kind of subversion and a sort of crime that requires punishment." The deputy head of the Egyptian Supreme Court did admit, however, that the punishment for apostasy was "controversial", and asserted that there was nothing in any Qur'anic text about it. This case highlights the use of double talk by some Muslim leaders when speaking to western audiences and indicates that majority Muslim public opinion in most countries still supports the apostasy law and is not ready for its reform.[104]

Such double talk is apparent also when Muslims are used by Western governments as apologists for Islam in order to combat Islamophobia in Western societies. Thus the Australian government Department of Immigration and Citizenship in 2004 produced a promotional booklet on Islam titled: *Muslim Australians: Their Beliefs, Practices and Institutions*, authored by Professor Abdullah Saeed of Melbourne University.[105] In a section dealing with Western stereotypes and misconceptions of Islam, the proposition that "People who leave Islam (apostates) will be killed", is listed as one such misconception. The booklet states Islamic teaching on apostasy thus:

> From a religious point of view, the Qur'an stipulates that "there is no compulsion in religion" (2:256), and a person can neither be forced to become a Muslim nor to stay in the religion. In the past, apostasy was often linked with state treason, and for that reason some Muslim rulers imposed the death penalty on apostates. Also, in some parts of the Muslim world today, the threat of punishment for apostasy exists and is often used as a political tool against people by their opponents. However, many Muslims argue that this is abusing a fundamental principle in Islam that each person answers only to God in regard to their faith or lack thereof.[106]

The author presents his own liberal view as the contemporary Muslim norm. The Western reader is left with the impression that Islam is and has always been a tolerant religion that guarantees religious freedom even to converts from Islam (apostates). The booklet does not explain that the traditional law of apostasy demands the death penalty and is based on shari'a, which in turn is founded not only on the Qur'an, but also on Muhammad's practice as recounted in the *hadith*. The same author, in a book he co-authored with Hassan

Saeed,[107] repeatedly argues that even in modern times the law of apostasy that demands the death penalty for those leaving Islam is still accepted as unchangeable and immutable by the majority of Muslims:

> The vast majority of Muslim scholars writing on the issue of apostasy today follow the pre-modern position on apostasy ... apostasy is prohibited and no Muslim is allowed to convert to another religion or commit any of the offences which would make them an apostate. Apostasy for these scholars is punishable by death.[108]

While he himself opposes this view, and explains that there are some Muslims today who oppose it, he accepts that its defenders are the dominant voice in Islam:

> Its defenders, however, dominate the debate by drawing on ideas and views expressed in pre-modern Islamic law. They are armed with what they consider to be supporting texts from the Qur'an and *hadith*, the views of pre-modern Muslim scholars as well as *fatwas* from conservative religious leaders today. This leaves opponents of apostasy largely defenceless against what appears to be unassailable and authoritative 'textual' evidence.[109]

Western perceptions of Islam as an intolerant religion seem to be having some impact on Muslim leaders who are worried about the image of Islam in the wider world. In April 2009, a conference on Islamic jurisprudence organised by the International Islamic Fiqh Academy (IIFA), an organ of the OIC, was held in Sharjah in the UAE. The delegates debated religious tolerance and freedom of expression in Islam, including the law of apostasy. Several scholars demanded a review of the punishment for apostates in the light of changing modern values. Others challenged their argument, saying that the original Islamic texts call for the killing of apostates, and that the only debate was over the length of time that must elapse before the execution. Some doubted the validity of the texts that are quoted in support of the killing of apostates. Others refused to countenance a lighter approach toward apostates in the name of freedom of religion. In conclusion, a six-man committee was appointed to study the question of apostasy and submit recommendations. It is not clear whether there will be a definite outcome from this committee, or whether it is simply a tactic to divert attention from the issue in the hope that it will soon be forgotten.[110]

The Application of the
Apostasy Law in the World Today

In the nineteenth century the Ottoman Empire came into closer contact with Europe. As a result of diplomatic contacts, and then of Western colonial rule, a process of secularisation and Westernisation began, and Islamic law was gradually phased out in some Islamic countries. They retained at most only certain aspects of shari'a, usually family law, as part of more secular legal systems. Many Muslim states had secular constitutions at independence. The death penalty for apostasy was rarely applied.

In recent years, however, the rapidly growing influence of Islamism has led to the reversal of this trend in a gradual process of Islamisation. Most Muslim nations have declared Islam to be their state religion, and many have declared shari'a to be the primary source of their law.[111] In Saudi Arabia shari'a is considered to be the nation's constitution, and the Islamic penal code has also been reintroduced in Iran, Sudan and parts of Pakistan, Somalia and Nigeria. The official introduction of this code is deeply symbolic, although its implementation varies to a remarkable degree depending on power relations between the centre and the periphery in each country as well as on different interpretations of the legal issues. (See below for more details.)

Many Muslim states have two totally different legal systems operating in parallel: the Western secular system and the Islamic shari'a one. The comparative weighting given to each system varies between different states. Most states with a mixed system and a written constitution guarantee freedom of religion and equality of treatment to all citizens, including those belonging to religious minorities, but in practice the authorities usually give Muslims more rights than non-Muslims.[112]

This practice might seem surprising given that most modern Muslim states have ratified international agreements on human rights, but they limit the application of these by subordinating them to Islamic shari'a. Human rights and the equality of all people before the law are thus conditioned by shari'a, which discriminates on the basis of religion. Islamists defend this stance by claiming that the Western understanding of human rights is based on a radically secular worldview and that human rights must be applied in culture-specific ways, respecting the deep religiosity of the Muslim world.[113]

In Muslim states religion is not usually a private matter, as in the West, but is under state control to a greater or lesser degree. Freedom of religion is understood in the Islamic way, i.e. as freedom of worship for officially recognised religious minorities within their communities. The individual freedom of choosing a religion is restricted to non-Muslims who choose Islam; Muslims are not allowed to choose another religion and, as shown above, for them to do so is regarded as a grave offence.

The incorporation of shari'a laws into the state legal system enables official charges to be made within the state courts against those accused of apostasy and/or blasphemy. Apostasy is punishable by death in Afghanistan, Iran, Mauritania, Saudi Arabia, North Sudan and Yemen, and it is also illegal or punishable in others such as the Comoros, Jordan, Kuwait, Malaysia and the Maldives.[114] In some countries, such as Morocco, the government regards all citizens as Muslims, so conversion from Islam is simply unrecognised. Official proceedings against those who reject Islam are fairly rare, partly because most keep their conversion a closely guarded secret, and the death penalty is still not often implemented. But increasingly severe punishments for the act of apostasy are being imposed, and it is common for apostates to be deprived of all their civil rights. Their marriages may be dissolved so that they lose their spouses and children, and their right of inheritance may be withdrawn.

A Muslim who leaves his or her faith is often viewed as guilty of treason and liable to the death penalty even if there is no official punishment for apostasy laid down in the constitution or legal system. Various methods can be used to punish or even kill apostates even if there is no applicable law on the statute books, for example, by framing them for other offences, or arresting them for causing public disorder because of the outcry about their conversion. Arrest can be followed by beatings, torture and imprisonment.

Where suitable legal provisions do not yet exist, or where state legal systems are not interested in pursuing apostates, the religious authorities may act on their own initiative to carry out what they see as obligatory shari'a penalties against those accused of apostasy. *Fatwas* may be issued either by state shari'a courts or by individual *'ulama*, demanding the death of the apostate, using the statement "His blood is permissible". Individual *fatwas* are not legally binding on the state but can be acted upon by any Muslim, and many would argue that an assassin is obeying shari'a and must not be prosecuted. The Civil Codes of several states, including Egypt, Algeria, Syria and Kuwait, allow the use of religious *fatwas* based on shari'a.[115]

If neither the state authorities nor the religious authorities act, converts may still suffer enormous social pressure and severe harassment, as their conversion is seen as a betrayal of Islam that brings great shame on family and community. Among the Muslim masses, apostasy is an emotive subject that easily provokes negative responses; it can also be manipulated by those who see themselves as defenders of traditional Islam or by those who could benefit from the downfall of accused people.

Many employers will dismiss converts from their jobs. Some relatives will try to have an apostate officially declared insane, as the insane are not held accountable for their actions.[116] Families exert pressure by coercive measures such as threats and violence, or by tearful pleading, urging converts to return to Islam. Some try to "wash away" the shame of apostasy by casting offenders out of the family, driving them out of the country or even killing them: a number of converts in several countries, including Egypt and Pakistan, have been murdered by enraged family members and friends. Mobs can be easily incited to launch frenzied attacks against offenders, their families and their communities, or individual Muslims zealous for their religion and its honour may take it on themselves to assassinate alleged apostates, believing that they are doing a holy service to God and to Islam.[117] The perpetrators are rarely prosecuted by the authorities and frequently go unpunished. Some Muslim states worry about the unwelcome attention given by the Western media to cases of apostasy, so they prefer to let such cases be handled unofficially by the community.

As we have seen, the term "apostate" (*murtadd*) usually refers to a Muslim who has officially converted to another faith, thus becoming a *kafir*. But others, who claim to be good Muslims, can also be accused of unbelief, blasphemy and heresy as well as of apostasy, for various other reasons including scepticism, atheism, ascribing partners or associates to God and not fully implementing shari'a. In some contemporary Muslim states traditional definitions of apostasy, blasphemy and heresy have been broadened to include anyone who disagrees with what the authorities, religious and/or governmental, consider to be orthodox Islam.[118] The shari'a laws on apostasy and blasphemy are increasingly being used by some states arbitrarily to detain citizens who are viewed with disfavour by the authorities (or by militant Muslims), and to suppress any idea, person or group that contradicts the established regime. In many cases multiple charges of apostasy, blasphemy, unbelief, heresy and insulting Islam and Muhammad are brought against those accused, thus giving the judges greater flexibility in deciding under which category to define the crime and ensuring that the defendants are convicted of something. A feature of accusations of apostasy and blasphemy is the way they are often uncritically accepted as true by members of the police and of the criminal justice system, who require little or no evidence.[119] The result is that Muslims themselves are increasingly in danger of suffering what is, in effect, murder by other Muslims. Even if members of Muslim minorities are not executed for holding views that the government considers heretical, they may suffer discrimination, harassment and imprisonment.[120]

Blasphemy and non-Muslims

While a charge of apostasy can be laid only against Muslims who leave Islam, a charge of blasphemy is applicable to non-Muslims as well. According to the law of blasphemy anyone, of no matter what background or religion, who disparages Muhammad in any way, however slight, is liable to the death penalty.

Qadi' Ilyad referes specifically to non-Muslims:

> In The Book of Muhammad the Companions of Malik have told us that he said that whosoever curses the Messenger of Allah or any other Prophet, be he Muslim or unbeliever, is killed without being asked to repent ... As for the dhimmi who curses the

Prophet, says he is not a Prophet, was not sent by Allah or the Qur'an was not sent down upon him or that it is something he made up, he is killed.[121]

These quotes reveal how easy it is for anyone, Muslim or non-Muslim, to fall foul of the blasphemy law and how serious the consequences of any slip of the tongue can be.

The growth in Islam's power in the world is being accompanied by determined efforts to protect Islam from any critique or disparagement, which are regarded as blasphemy. Pressure by Muslims for the enactment of religious hatred laws is intended to be a step towards the international implementation of shari'a blasphemy law.

In 2008, at the 11th Session of the Islamic Summit Conference held in Dakar, (13-14 March 2008), Resolution No.11/11-C (Is) "On the Defamation of Religions and Discrimination Against Muslims" was passed, which stated among other things:

> **Alarmed** at the burgeoning tide of Islamophobia in certain non-Islamic countries and increasing incidences of acts of discrimination against Muslims on the basis of religion, and **noting with concern** the inaction by some non-Islamic states to combat the defamation of religions, including Islam, and discriminatory practices against Muslims, **Condemning** all forms of defamation of religions and strongly condemning the republishing of the abhorrent and reprehensible caricatures of Prophet Muhammad (PBUH) and all other incidents of the defamation or desecration of the Holy symbols of Islam,
>
> 1. **Strongly deplores** all acts of violence and assaults, and incitement thereto, against persons on the basis of their religion, and all acts of violence directed against Holy symbols or sites or places of worship of all religions, and express deep concern at the intensification of the campaign of defamation of religions, particularly against Islam;
>
> 2. **Asserts** that acts of defamation of all religions, including Islam, represent violations of the human rights of the followers of those religions, and emphasizes that discriminations between the persons on grounds of religions constitutes an affront to human

dignity and a disavowal of the fundamental freedoms and basic human rights afforded to all persons;

11.Urges all states, in light of their obligations to respect, protect and fulfill human rights, to undertake the following measures to combat the defamation of religions and to protect the adherents of religions against discrimination;

The Resolution called on all states to:

Ensure the criminalization of all acts of defamation of religions and discrimination on the basis of religion, and to enact the appropriate penalties that represent adequate deterrence against such practices;

It also issued instructions to its delegation at the UNHRC:

Requests the OIC Group within the United Nations Human Rights Council to endeavor to adopt an international instrument on the prohibition of the defamation of religions and to declare such practices as a violation of human rights and fundamental freedoms.

The Final Communiqué of the "Annual Coordination Meeting of Ministers of Foreign Affairs of The OIC Member States" at the United Nations Headquarters, New York, on 26 September 2008 stated that:

The Meeting condemned the growing trend of Islamophobia and systematic discrimination against Muslims. It called upon the international community to prevent incitement to hatred and discrimination against Muslims and take effective measures to combat defamation of religions and acts of negative stereotyping of people based on religion, belief or ethnicity. The Meeting requested the Secretary General to continue the OIC initiatives to effectively counter Islamophobia through discussion and debates at various international fora and stressed the importance that Member States continue their support to the organization's observatory on Islamophobia.

Also:

The Meeting emphasized the fact that defamation of religions constitutes a form of incitement to religious hatred, hostility and violence against the followers of these religions which in turn leads to the denial of their fundamental rights and freedoms. It further stressed that combating religious discrimination in general requires a particular focus on preventing the direct and indirect consequences of defamation of religions, including its role in legitimizing discriminatory discourse and ideological violence.

Demands for the worldwide protection of religions from incitement to hatred and violence are also being made at the UN. The driving force is the 57 Muslim states united in the OIC and especially its member states Pakistan, Saudi Arabia and Iran. The campaigners believe that the Qur'an, the *hadith*, the shari'a and Muhammad must be protected from any criticism, however factual. Their goal is to give Islam a privileged place, not granted to other religions, within the public sphere in all societies. Because in Islam there is no separation of religion from the state, they see the state as the guarantor and protector of Islam, and they expect the UN, which represents all states in the world, to fulfil the same function. This expectation contradicts the basic Western principles of free thought and expression, and also "the right to freedom of opinion and expression" enshrined in Article 19 of the Universal Declaration of Human Rights.

The power of the OIC and of individual Muslim states is also being marshalled to promote UN resolutions to protect Islam from perceived criticism and offences. This campaign is seen as a prelude to the introduction of legislative changes favourable to Islam in Western and other non-Muslim states. Muslim communities in the West often pressure governments and legislatures by complaining about Islamophobia and requesting laws to protect Islam.

The UN increasingly practises self-censorship to counter accusations of "blasphemy", "Islamophobia", "defamation of Islam", or "sacrilege". For the sake of political and diplomatic advantage, many states seem willing to accept the new rules being requested by the OIC. The constant pressure, and the resolutions adopted at the UN, have served to restrict open discussions of matters not congenial to Muslim states, such as slavery in Sudan or Muslim anti-Semitism. Discussion about political issues within Islamic states is now out of bounds, and freedom of speech and expression is being eroded in many international organisations and conferences.[122] Non-Muslim states seem to have decided to keep silent on topics relating to Islam, thus conforming to the demands of Islamic shari'a.[123]

Representatives of Muslim states have requested, and to some extent received, special treatment, especially in the Commission on Human Rights (UNCHR) and its successor, the UN Human Rights Council (UNHRC).[124] The "representatives of Islam", especially the OIC, have an unprecedented exceptional status at the UN.

Pressure has been building in the UN in recent years specifically to forbid the defamation of Islam. As a result, terms such as "blasphemy" and "defamation of Islam" have appeared in UN documents. Since 2005 the UN General Assembly has introduced annual resolutions against the defamation of religions,[125] and in 2007 one of these was passed for the first time.[126] The OIC is seeking to attain UN support and legitimation of Islamic shari'a-based anti-blasphemy prohibitions, and their incorporation into international human rights law. At present "defamation of religions" has no basis in international human rights law, but it is likely soon to have one if the Muslim states keep up their campaign.[127]

As a result of Islamic pressures, on 6 March 2008 the UN General Assembly adopted a resolution (62/154) combating the defamation of religion. It expressed "deep concern about the negative stereotyping of religions and manifestations of intolerance and discrimination in matters of religion or belief". It specifically mentioned Islam in four of its 18 points, expressing "deep concern that Islam is frequently and wrongly associated with human rights violations and terrorism", noting "the intensification of the campaign of defamation of religions and the ethnic and religious profiling of Muslim minorities in the aftermath of the tragic events of 11 September 2001", and deploring all "means to incite acts of violence, xenophobia or related intolerance and discrimination against Islam or any other religion"; it also stressed the "need to effectively combat defamation of all religions and incitement to religious hatred against Islam and Muslims in particular". The resolution also urged all states to provide legal protection against acts of hatred resulting from the defamation of religions.[128]

In March 2009, Pakistan, on behalf of the OIC, circulated a draft resolution at a session of the UNHRC entitled "Combating Defamation of Religions". It repeated much of what was contained in the March 2008 resolution and specifically mentioned Islam and Muslims but no other religious community. Its aim was to ban any perceived offence to Islam. It called on states to harmonise actions at all levels, local, national and international, to combat defamation of religion and protect citizens by legal and constitutional means against acts arising out of it. At the time of writing the resolution had not been adopted, but given that Islamic states dominate the UNHRC with the support of non-democratic members such as Russia, China and Cuba, it was expected to pass.[129]

The OIC is seeking international legitimation of its own state-sanctioned blasphemy laws, which stifle religious freedom, subject religious minorities to persecution and outlaw conversions from Islam to other faiths. The first victims of its campaign are likely to be moderate Muslims and religious minorities in states such as Pakistan, Iran, Sudan and Saudi Arabia, which support the resolutions. Other victims will be writers, journalists and intellectuals in the democratic West, who will be targeted for the "deliberate stereotyping of religions, their adherents and sacred persons".

Should these trends continue, there will be no need in the future for *fatwas* such as the one issued by Ayatollah Khomeini demanding the death of Salman Rushdie. Non-Muslim states will themselves prosecute their own citizens for alleged "blasphemy" against Muhammad and Islam. Following the above-mentioned UN resolutions, it may well be that the International Court of Justice will also be empowered to prosecute "offenders" internationally.

Apostasy, Christian mission, and the jihadi nexus

Both Christianity and Islam are missionary religions. While Muslims are free to propagate Islam in the West, however, most Muslim states severely restrict Christian mission or completely forbid it. At the same time most Muslims are convinced that Christianity can win converts from Islam only by using underhand methods, inducements and subtle pressure. For many Muslims, apostasy is linked to a subliminal fear of Christian mission and the expansion of Christianity and to resentment regarding the Crusades and of colonialism. Christianity is seen as an illegitimate competitor to Islam on a global level in the modern world, and Christian mission is seen as a challenge to Islam that demands a resolute response, including the application of the death penalty for converts to Christianity. Preventing conversions and punishing converts also becomes a matter of protecting the honour of Islam and the Islamic *umma*. According to Abdullah and Hassan Saeed:

> The ghost of Christianity lurks behind the Muslim debates on Islam and the West, Westernization, secularization and even the debate on apostasy.[130]

The fear of Christianisation (often linked in Muslim minds to Westernisation, secularisation and globalisation) and the impact of traditional anti-apostasy rhetoric has seen the establishment of many anti-apostasy organisations dedicated to fighting legal Christian missionary activities. These easily become radicalised and mutate from non-violent groups to jihadi-linked groups engaged in indiscriminate violence against all Christians, including indigenous Christians. The outrage many feel at conversions to Christianity can easily be exploited by groups with a jihadi agenda. A recent example from Indonesia involves a Palembang, South Sumatra branch of an Islamic anti-apostasy organisation, Forum Against Conversion Movement (Forum Gerakan Pemurtadan, FAKTA). This small local group, whose biggest concern was the conversion of Muslims by Christian evangelicals, was infiltrated by two jihadis linked to the violent Jemaah Islamiyah (JI) and the Noordin Network. They soon radicalised the group and convinced them of the legitimacy of using violence against converts, missionaries and Christians in general to achieve their aims. The group killed a Christian schoolteacher who was also a pastor, and was planning further, more ambitious attacks when ten of its members were arrested in April 2009 by the authorities.[131]

Practice in Muslim nations

Saudi Arabia[132]

In Saudi Arabia the Qur'an is the state constitution and shari'a the legal system. The strict Wahhabi interpretation prohibits the public practice of any other religion than Islam in the Arabian Peninsula, and this is applied within Saudi territory. Even private practice can provoke harassment by the religious police, arrests and deportation, with harsher treatment for non-Westerners than for Westerners.

Offences are regulated by a mixture of shari'a rules and government-legislated laws, most of which are extremely vague and therefore open to abuse. In categorising offences and deciding punishments, judges are guided by vaguely worded laws and general principles of Islamic jurisprudence that are subject to different interpretations by different jurists. For example, it is the judge who decides what constitutes apostasy. In a 1992 case brought against a Saudi Shi'a Muslim, 'Abd al-Karim Mal al-Allah, it was reported that the judge told the accused, "Abandon your rejectionist beliefs or I will kill you." The discretionary powers of the judge are further enhanced by the secrecy of court proceedings, which protects judges from legal challenges by defence lawyers.

In Saudi Arabia only the state is allowed to make declarations on issues such as the death penalty. Anyone who starts a debate on the subject is likely to be branded an apostate or one of the "corrupt on earth", and both kinds of offender are themselves liable to capital punishment.

A young Saudi woman called Fatima al-Mutairi learned about Jesus Christ on the internet and decided to follow Him. But in 2008 her family discovered her faith, and a male relative cut out her tongue and then burned her to death. It is apparently being considered an "honour crime", and the killer may therefore receive a relatively lenient sentence.

Pakistan[133]

In Pakistan, apostasy is not punishable by the country's Penal Code, despite its being a capital offence in shari'a. Blasphemy, however, which according to shari'a is a lesser crime, is a capital offence under the Penal Code.

As part of a gradual trend towards Islamisation, severe amendments were added in 1982 (section 295-B) and 1986 (section 295-C) to Section 295 of the Penal Code, often called the "Blasphemy Law". Under these new provisions, desecration of the Qur'an became a crime carrying a punishment of life imprisonment (295-B), while defiling the name of Muhammad became a crime incurring the death penalty or imprisonment for life and a fine (295-C). In 1990 the Federal Shari'at Court ruled that the penalty for defiling the name of Muhammad "is death and nothing else". This declaration invalidated the words "punishment for life" in section 295-C, making the death penalty mandatory for this offence.[134]

As a result of these legal changes, the number of blasphemy cases brought to court has increased dramatically. The main targets of the law have been the minority groups, especially Ahmadis[135] and Christians. The well known Pakistani scholar Akbar S. Ahmed states that in the last decade some 2,000 Ahmadis have been charged, and some 60 Christians a year.[136] But Muslims have also been accused in significant numbers.

Blasphemy legislation has become a weapon in personal disputes: unscrupulous people can now manipulate it to their advantage, knowing the great emotional impact of the charges on most Muslims, including the judges and jurors. In fact the majority of accusations are made by people bearing a personal grudge against others for reasons that have nothing to do with religion. Many cases originate because of professional jealousy and rivalry or the quest for economic gain. Ahmed says that in recent years the blasphemy laws have been used increasingly for settling political vendettas and land disputes.[137] The accuser has nothing to lose, while the accused might lose everything, including his or her life.

Bail is usually denied to those charged with blasphemy, while trials are expensive and can take years to begin. In accordance with Islamic law, courts tend to believe the testimony of Muslims over that of Christians. One judge, finding a Christian guilty of blasphemy on the testimony of a single witness from a militant Muslim group, said, "Sajjad Hussain is a young man of 21 years of age, a student of the fourth year, with a beard and the outlook of a true Muslim, and I have no reason to disbelieve him."[138] Defence lawyers and judges dealing with blasphemy cases are often threatened.[139] Although the higher courts have tended to acquit people accused of blasphemy, on appeal and following long periods in detention, the state security services have frequently failed to protect the rights of the accused afterwards. Many find themselves under attack by extremist groups.[140]

The laws seriously intimidate non-Muslim minorities and Muslim opposition or reform movements by creating an atmosphere in which threats, individual and mob violence and extremist terrorist acts against non-Muslims are seen as acceptable and are even supported by the state and its law enforcers. As a result they encourage private violence against presumed apostates by Muslims zealous for their religion, and religious leaders can easily whip a crowd into a murderous frenzy by spurious allegations of blasphemy, apostasy and insults against Muhammad.

It is of interest to note that when Benazir Bhutto, then leader of the opposition, criticized the Shari'at Court in 1992 for increasing the severity of the penalties for blasphemy, the Federal Minister for Religious Affairs, Mawlana Abadu Sitar Niazi, issued a *fatwa* against her declaring her to be a *kafir* liable to the death penalty. A year later, when she was Prime Minister, a case was brought against her in the Lahore High Court under Section 295-C by Zia ul-Islam, leader of the Pakistan Movement for Workers, accusing her of criticising the blasphemy law. This case illustrates how the law can be manipulated against almost anyone, and while powerful figures might be able to defend themselves, ordinary citizens (especially members of minority groups) are cowed into silence and live in a climate of constant fear and insecurity.[141]

Soon after he seized power, General Pervez Musharraf tried in 2000 to alter the law to allow an inquiry by district officials into any blasphemy complaint before police could arrest a suspect, but he had to withdraw his amendment under pressure from Islamic hardliners.[142] Since then there have been other attempts to challenge the legislation, including the proposal by various human rights groups in 2004 of a law to punish "false" blasphemy claims. So far these attempts at reform have been unsuccessful, though a minister in the new civilian government has recently announced that the blasphemy law will be abolished.

Egypt[143]

The Egyptian constitution of 1923 guaranteed the equality before the law of all Egyptians, without distinction of race, religion or language. In 1971, however, the Supreme Constitutional Tribunal approved a law that stated: "Islam is the State religion and any law contrary to Islam is contrary to the Constitution." Apostasy is not directly forbidden in the constitution; nor is it officially restricted or penalised. But the declaration in the amended constitution of 1981 (article 2, see endnote 9) that shari'a is the main source of legislation opened the door to the prosecution of apostates.

There are several rulings by the Supreme Administrative Court and the Court of Cassation that Muslims who apostatise are to be considered legally dead and to lose all civil rights and powers, including their marriage and inheritance rights. They lose custody of their children; they cannot withdraw funds from their bank accounts; they cannot have their religion changed on their identity cards or other legal documentation. They are thus left unprotected against harassment and persecution by state institutions and wider society.

Article 98F of the penal code prohibits contempt for religion, disturbance of public order, and endangering social peace. Because these are offences that threaten national security and unity, those accused are tried before the State Security Courts, which are responsible for the state's emergency laws, rather than by the civil courts. Many converts have been arrested and detained under this legislation without specific charge, on the grounds that converts threaten social peace and inter-communal relations, and have been detained in maximum-security prisons. Some have been brutally tortured.[144]

Since the 1970s Muslim conservatives in Egypt have been demanding a reinstatement of the death penalty for apostasy. Many objections have been raised by the Christian minority, liberal Muslims and secular elements in Egyptian society, and the government has so far resisted the conservative demands, which nevertheless continue.[145]

The growing influence of Islamists over the last two decades has encouraged groups such as al-Jama'a al-Islamiyya to mount campaigns of *takfir* against intellectuals and artists. These have led to some violent attacks and even to assassination. Sheikh Muhammad al-Ghazali, an influential theologian, issued a *fatwa* legitimising the shedding of the blood of anyone who opposed the application of shari'a.

Islamist groups and lawyers have also sought to force the divorce of liberal-secularists of Muslim heritage who have made what are considered to be "apostate" statements, and of couples in which one member has converted from Islam. They do so using the legal tool of *hisba*, which is based on an Islamic teaching that each Muslim has the responsibility to enforce "Islamic behaviour" in his or her society. Where one member deviates from this conduct, every Muslim is offended and therefore has a direct legal interest, allowing him or her to bring a charge against the offender.

The influential Al-Azhar Islamic University and its Islamic Research Academy (IRA) are officially authorised by the Government to safeguard Islamic law and religion. As a result, Al-Azhar has exercised ever more stringent censorship over books, the media and the arts, banning and confiscating many items and accusing their authors of blasphemy or apostasy.[146]

Interestingly, the Al-Azhar Creed and Philosophy Committee, which is affiliated to the IRA, recently recommended a change in the application of the apostasy law, suggesting that the accused person should be given a whole lifetime to renounce apostasy instead of the three-day period laid down in Islamic jurisprudence (*fiqh*). This recommendation was severely criticised by many religious leaders as a forbidden innovation (*bid'a*).[147]

Sudan

President Nimeiri introduced shariʿa law in Sudan in 1983, provoking a renewal of the civil war between the Islamic government in the north of the country and the predominantly Christian population in the south. In 1985 Mahmoud Muhammad Taha, an Islamic scholar and leader of the Republican Brothers movement, was condemned to death as an apostate and executed for his efforts to reform Islam and reinterpret the Qur'an in a liberal direction. Following the military coup of 1989 led by Omar al-Bashir the National Islamic Front led by Hassan al-Turabi came to power, and in the constitution of 1991 the Islamic Code was again enforced, effectively establishing Sudan as an Islamic state. The use of shariʿa as the basis of law and government has since become more explicit.[148]

While the 1998 constitution proclaims religious freedom for all citizens, it also claims that Islamic shariʿa is a source of the country's legislation.[149] In practice the government treats Islam as the state religion and declares that it must inspire the nation's laws, institutions and policies. Non-Muslims are forbidden to proselytise, and section 126 of the Sudan Criminal Law of 1991 makes apostasy from Islam a criminal offence punishable by death in accordance with shariʿa.[150] Although this extreme penalty is seldom implemented, apostates face arrest, imprisonment and torture. Representatives of the Sudanese government claim that apostasy is not punishable as such, but that any manifestation of it in public constitutes a threat to public order and should be prosecuted as high treason.[151]

The 2005 peace agreement that ended the civil war also resulted in an Interim National Constitution that was significantly different from the previous one:

> Although the 2005 Interim National Constitution (INC) provides for freedom of religion throughout the entire country, the INC enshrines Shari'a as a source of legislation in the north, and the official laws and policies of the Government favor Islam in the north. The Constitution of Southern Sudan provides for freedom of religion in the south, and other laws and policies of the Government of South Sudan (GoSS) contributed to the generally free practice of religion ... Although there is no penalty for converting from another religion to Islam, converting from Islam to another religion is punishable by imprisonment and even death in the north; however, a death sentence for apostasy has

never been carried out by the current Government ... Muslims in the north who express an interest in Christianity or convert to Christianity faced severe social pressure to recant.[152]

Iran

Since the 1979 Iranian revolution Shi'a Islam has been the state religion of Iran, and shari'a has formed the basis of its constitution and legal system. Article 4 of the constitution states that "All civil, penal financial, economic, administrative, cultural, military, political, and other laws and regulations must be based on Islamic criteria. This principle applies absolutely and generally to all articles of the Constitution as well as to all other laws and regulations ..." While the state recognizes Christianity, Judaism and Zoroastrianism as official religions and gives limited freedom to their adherents to worship within their own communities, Islamic "heretics" such as the Baha'is face severe persecution as unprotected infidels.

Although Article 23 of the constitution guarantees freedom of belief ("[t]he investigation of individuals' beliefs is forbidden, and no one may be molested or taken to task simply for holding a certain belief"), various laws restrict religious liberty. These restrictive and often contradictory laws are found in the Penal Code, the Theologians' Law (a body of law dealing with offences committed by clerics) and the Public and Revolutionary Courts' Procedural Law. A basic flaw in many of these laws is the absence of clear definitions of key concepts such as "state security", "propaganda" and "insulting Islam". Under Article 513 of the Penal Code offences classified as "insult to religion" can be punishable by death or prison terms of between one and five years. Articles 6 and 26 of the Press Code forbid writings "containing apostasy and matters against Islamic standards [and] 'the true religion of Islam' ..." In cases where there are no specific codified laws to cover the particular issue under consideration, judges are permitted by Article 167 of the constitution to deliver verdicts based on authoritative Islamic sources and *fatwas*.[153]

In recent years many people who have expressed their conscientiously held beliefs have been detained, tried and imprisoned under these laws.[154] Using their right to deliver judgments based on Islamic sources, judges have sentenced a number of converts from Islam to death, and one was executed in 1990 (see below).

On 2 September 2008, the Iranian Parliament provisionally approved a bill that mandates the death penalty for any male Muslim who converts from Islam to another religion, and lifelong imprisonment for female converts from Islam. At the time of writing the bill is being reviewed in parliament, and MPs have the opportunity to amend it; it also has to be vetted by the Council of Guardians, a twelve-member legislative body that has the power to veto any bill that does not conform to Islamic law and the constitution. If passed, it will introduce the death penalty for apostasy into Iranian law itself, so that judges no longer have to resort to Islamic law in order to pass death sentences on those who have left Islam.

Malaysia

Malaysia has a complex legal system that combines Islamic Syariah law (as shari'a law is called in Malaysia) and *adat* (local, customary or traditional law) with a quasi-secular constitution and common law. Parts of Syariah law relating to family and religious matters are binding on Muslims. There is continuing debate in Malaysia about which form of law should have supremacy in respect of religious freedom. Malaysia is a Muslim-majority country, with ethnic Malays, who are officially reckoned as Muslim, comprising some 50% of the population.

The constitution declares Islam to be the official state religion while guaranteeing religious freedom. A 1993 bill states, however, that it is illegal for a Muslim to change religion. The constitution allows state legislatures to restrict the propagation of any non-Islamic religious teaching among Muslims in their jurisdiction. Most states have in fact enacted laws forbidding the propagation of other religions among Muslims, making it an offence to persuade, influence or incite a Muslim to change his or her religion. Non-Muslims are even forbidden to use certain Islamic Arabic terms such as Allah, *ulama*, *hadith*, *syariah* and similar terms in their publications.[155]

Malays are given a superior status as the original indigenous peoples of the country (*bumiputera*),[156] and they are given many political and economic advantages over non-Malays. In the decades since independence, these advantages have become enshrined further in law and in programmes of affirmative action.[157] The legal definition of "Malay" includes being a Muslim, so Malays who convert from Islam lose their ethnic identity and all its associated privileges in addition to suffering the legal penalties.[158]

There has been pressure to make Malaysia a fully Islamic state, particularly by the opposition Islamist Party of Malaysia (PAS). As a result, Malaysia has experienced significant Islamisation, and in 2001 it was proclaimed an Islamic country.[159]

PAS has also been pressurising Parliament to pass a law imposing the death sentence for apostasy. While under PAS control, two states, Kelantan (1993) and Terengganu (2002), passed *hudud* laws (i.e. criminal laws under Syariah) that would punish apostasy from Islam with the death penalty. The federal government has prevented the implementation of such laws, however.[160] The former Prime Ministers Mahathir Mohamad and Abdullah Badawi have also opposed all attempts to pass such a law at the federal level. According to the Malaysian constitution, while Syariah courts are under state, not federal control, criminal law is a federal matter. Unless the constitution is amended, the local *hudud* laws cannot be applied.

Various Malaysian states have nevertheless passed laws targeting apostates. Under these laws, those declared to be apostates by a Syariah court are forced to attend an Islamic Faith Rehabilitation Centre for counselling and re-education for more than six months. If they then say they are still not Muslims they will be further detained. This policy is supported by the federal government. Most states have also criminalised the propagation to Muslims of religions other than Islam.

Although PAS was critically weakened following its failure in the 2004 General Election and also lost control of Terengganu state, calls for a strengthening of Malaysia's Islamic identity have not stopped. Some civil rights groups have seen recent cases on apostasy as important in the struggle against Islamisation. It should be noted that the members of these groups are often themselves Muslims. One activist, Haris Mohamed Ibrahim, explained the position as follows: "Apostasy is not a new phenomenon but the issue has come to the forefront because it underscores the growing Islamisation of a country that was intended to be secular." The brave "Sisters in Islam" movement has also struggled against the imposition of Syariah and *hudud* laws at both federal and state levels.[161]

Maldives [162]

This small island nation is a staunch bastion of Islam. The country is spread across 1,200 coral atolls and islands, with a population of 380,000, most with South Indian, Sinhalese, and Arab roots. The Maldives, like Saudi Arabia, legally allows only one faith, Sunni Islam, to be practised publicly. All citizens must be Muslims, and the public practice of any other faith is forbidden.[163]

A new Constitution of the Republic of Maldives was ratified by the then President Maumoon Abdul Gayoom on 7 August 2008. It introduced some key liberal and democratic reforms, such as the separation of powers and a bill of rights. The former restrictions on religious freedom have been tightened, however. The new constitution spells out more strongly than the old that all Maldivians have to be Muslims and states that "no law contrary to any tenet of Islam shall be enacted in the Maldives". Article 9, Section D states that "a non-Muslim may not become a citizen of the Maldives". The Information Minister had warned on his personal blog that "When the revised constitution gets introduced, it will operate to take away the citizenship from citizens of Maldives who may have a faith different from Islam." This statement implies not only that some 3,000 non-Muslim Maldivians will lose their citizenship but also that Maldivians who convert from Islam to another faith will do so.[164] They will be allowed to stay in the country and work, but they will be stripped of citizen rights such as freedom of speech, freedom of movement and habeas corpus.

In the past, Maldivians suspected of having converted to another faith have been imprisoned, and publicly branded as traitors, second class citizens and immature. They were also accused of having been led astray by "foreign forces". Converts were released only after signing a declaration that they believed in Islam. After their release, they were shunned and regarded with suspicion by government officials and the general public, and some lost their jobs. Nonetheless, recent press reports claim that some of the country's vibrant blogging community have identified themselves as atheists or Christians.[165]

In June 2008 the Maldives banned a book, "Freedom of Religion, Apostasy and Islam", written by their former attorney general Hassan Saeed and his brother, Melbourne University professor Abdullah Saeed. This questions the validity of the apostasy law in Islam and advocates reform.[166]

President Gayoom had ruled for thirty years, but the October 2008 elections were won by Mohamed Nasheed, a former Amnesty

International prisoner of conscience who has spent long periods in jail for constantly criticising the previous regime. It is hoped that he will develop a more liberal policy on religious freedom.[167]

Who is targeted?

As can be seen from the examination of Islamic teaching and practice above, accusations of apostasy, blasphemy, heresy and all other forms of *kufr* are aimed at several categories of people in Islamic and Western societies:

1. Muslims who have converted to another faith (e.g. to Christianity) or no faith

2. Muslim intellectuals who are believed to be deviating from traditional interpretations (reformers, secularists, modernists, journalists, political opponents)

3. Sectarian groups within Islam, such as the Baha'i in Iran or the Ahmadis in Pakistan

4. Non-Muslim Westerners who are perceived to have insulted Islam

Some case studies

The world media, Human Rights NGOs, Christian organisations and non-Muslim minority groups report many instances of the application of apostasy and blasphemy laws. A small representative sample of such cases will serve to illustrate how these laws operate.

1. Converts from Islam in Muslim-Majority Countries

KUWAIT

Hussein Ali Qambar

In late 1995 Hussein Ali Qambar, a Kuwaiti Shi'a building contractor, converted to Christianity and became a member of an expatriate evangelical church. Qambar's apostasy became publicly known following a custody dispute with his wife, from whom he had separated some months before. The court had given the mother custody of the children while the father had the right to see them on Fridays. Qambar's wife refused him this right and when asked for the reason declared in court that it was in order to protect the children as her husband had converted to Christianity.

Qambar did not go into hiding and did not practise the usual secrecy of converts from Islam. He met with the press, wearing a silver cross round his neck, and declared that he had "found God elsewhere". Following Islamic law, a group of *ulama* met several times with Qambar to persuade him to return to Islam. When he refused these advances popular anger started rising against him. In January 1996 an Islamist deputy in the National Assembly called for legal action against him. Soon afterwards, three independent Islamist lawyers filed a suit against Qambar requesting that he be declared an apostate and be stripped of his civil rights. Meanwhile his home was vandalised (probably by Ministry of the Interior officials); he was barred from seeing his children; and when his father died he was forbidden from receiving his share of the inheritance. On 24 April 1996 at a hearing before the Islamic court the prosecution called for Qambar to be stripped of his nationality and civil rights for offending against Islamic law by abandoning his Islamic faith. On 29 May 1996 a judge in the shari'a lower court issued a ruling officially declaring Qambar an apostate and recommending the death penalty, while also ordering him to pay the costs of the case. The presiding judge, Ja'far al-Mazidi, was later asked by the press if the ruling could be taken as permission to kill Qambar, and he replied, "That is possible," but that killing an apostate would be a violation of Kuwaiti criminal law. He added that there was no legal penalty for apostasy under Kuwait's criminal law, but there was such a penalty under shari'a. The court also made it clear that it understands there to be a difference between religious freedom and the freedom to convert from Islam to another faith. The accused had openly confessed to his conversion, thus giving the court all the evidence it needed.

Qambar appealed against the ruling to the Court of Appeal and the first hearing was scheduled for 15 September 1996. One month before that date, the authorities issued him a passport and he left Kuwait for the USA. He later reconverted to Islam and returned to Kuwait.

In Kuwait both traditionalist and liberal wings of the population were remarkably united in condemning Qambar. All agreed that his apostasy was a serious crime which had to be punished, and that depriving him of all his civil rights was legitimate. Some on the traditional side kept calling for the death penalty to be implemented.

Qambar's defence rested on a universalist discourse based on Western notions of human rights and citizenship. He referred to the Universal Declaration of Human Rights, which calls for freedom of religion, as well as to articles in the Kuwaiti Constitution (29 and 35) that guarantee freedom of belief. Article 35 reads: "Freedom of belief is absolute. The state protects the freedom of practicing religion in accordance with established customs, provided it does not conflict with public policy or morals." This article is obviously open to various interpretations: on the one hand, freedom of religion is absolute; on the other hand, it is limited by custom and morals.

Most Kuwaitis, however, appealed to traditional Muslim discourses of communal identity, reacting with anger against Qambar for betraying the Muslim community (*umma*), the Arab nation and the Kuwaiti community, and for being a tool of Western imperialist plots against Islam. They could not believe that he had converted for reasons of personal conviction. Liberal Kuwaitis accepted his being stripped of his civil rights as a just punishment, and no one from the most liberal sections of Kuwaiti society defended him.

This case demonstrates that even in a relatively liberal, modern and democratic Muslim state a majority of Muslims may still be unable to accept individuals' right to follow their inner conviction and conscience by changing their religion. All segments of the population united in condemning Qambar's conversion as betrayal, treason and apostasy worthy of the most severe penalties.

SUDAN

Alladin Omer Ajjabna Mohammed

When Alladin Omer Ajjabna Mohammed became a Christian in 1991 he was expelled from university and disowned by his family. In 2001, when he tried to go abroad to study, the local Muslim authorities learned that he was an apostate, and he was forcibly deported back to Sudan. He was arrested at Khartoum airport and charged with apostasy. Held incommunicado, he was tortured and ordered to return to Islam. He was released in September 2001 on medical grounds but had to report daily to the security forces. While reporting as required he disappeared again on 26 September 2001. On 30 January 2002, security police stopped Alladin from boarding a flight to Uganda where he planned to pursue theological studies. Though his papers were in order he was told that the computer system identified him as a criminal. While detained he was forcibly injected with unknown drugs. He attempted to fly out of Sudan again on 3 February 2002 but was again detained and ordered to report daily to the security police. He has now gone into hiding and the authorities have mounted an extensive manhunt for him. Sudanese Church authorities say there are a number of other former Muslims in a similar plight.[168]

Mekki Kuku[169]

Mekki Kuku is a Muslim primary school teacher from the Nuba Mountains, the father of ten children. He converted to Christianity and was charged in Khartoum with violating the Sudanese law on apostasy.

Kuku was arrested in Khartoum in June 1998 on charges of having violated Sudan's apostasy law. It was reported that he was tortured in jail and that he was offered financial rewards if he gave up his Christian faith. Following the intervention of Abel 'Alier, a former Vice-President of Sudan and leader of the opposition to Sudan's National Islamic Front (NIF), the torture sessions were suspended, and Kuku was transferred to Omdurman prison to await his trial. He suffered a stroke while in detention and was then released. He left Sudan for health reasons.

IRAN

Hossein Soodmand

The Reverend Hossein Soodmand was a Muslim who converted to Christianity in 1964 and acted as pastor and evangelist in the Assemblies of God church in Mashhad. He was arrested in 1989 and charged with apostasy and insulting Islam through his own conversion and by his efforts to convert other Muslims. He was sentenced to death by a Revolutionary Court in Mashhad, and despite pleas for clemency by fellow pastors to the Muslim cleric acting as Ombudsman, the *Dayro-e-Tasalamat* (literally, "he who hears the cries of the oppressed"), he was executed by hanging on 3 December 1990.[170]

Mehdi Dibaj

The Reverend Mehdi Dibaj, a Muslim who had converted to Christianity and was a minister of an Assemblies of God church in Babol, was arrested in 1983 and held for almost ten years without trial on charges of apostasy and insulting Islam. During that time, he was held for two years in solitary confinement and was subjected to mock executions. In December 1993 he was sentenced to death by a Revolutionary Court in Sari. Following much international pressure, Dibaj was released from prison in January 1994. On 20 June 1994, after attending a Christian conference in Karaj, he disappeared without a trace. On 5 July 1994, the Tehran police reported that his body had been found in a forest west of Tehran. The authorities denied the family's request for an independent autopsy, and he was buried on 13 July 1994.[171]

Hamid Pourmand

Hamid Pourmand, a colonel in the Iranian army, converted from Islam to Christianity before the 1979 Islamic Revolution. He was arrested by security forces in 2004 and has been held in detention ever since. Initially he was tried for apostasy and could have faced the death penalty, but the charge was dropped owing to international pressure. Instead he was given a three year jail sentence for "deceiving the army about his religion". Pourmand was convicted even though his lawyers had produced documents from the army that proved they had known about his conversion before promoting him to a higher rank. He has suffered psychological torture in prison, including being told several times to pack his clothes because he is about to be hanged.

Ghorban Tori

Ghorban Tori was a convert from Islam to Christianity who had converted many other Muslims. On 22 November 2005 he was kidnapped by security forces, and a few hours later he was found stabbed to death in front of his home in Gonbad-e-Kavus in north-eastern Iran. Following his murder the security services raided the houses of all the known Christians in the city.

YEMEN

Muhammad Haj Omar[172]

Muhammad Haj Omar is a Somali who settled in Yemen as a refugee in 1994 with his wife and infant son. He converted to Christianity in 1998 and changed his name to George. He was then arrested by the police on charges of apostasy. During his imprisonment he was beaten and threatened with death unless he returned to Islam. On 5 July 2000 a Yemeni court sentenced him to death by the sword for apostasy. He appealed against the sentence, and following the publicising of the case in the West by religious rights groups he was deported from Yemen and granted asylum in New Zealand.

PAKISTAN

Tahir Iqbal[173]

Tahir Iqbal was a Muslim who worked as a mechanic for the Pakistan Air Force. In 1984 his lower limbs became paralysed, and he had to retire from his job. At around that time he converted to Christianity and was baptised.

On 7 December 1990 a First Information Report (FIR) was filed against him by Peerzada 'Ali Ahmed Sabir. He was immediately arrested, and he was imprisoned in Kokhlapat Central Jail on 19 July 1992.

The accusation stated: that Iqbal had converted from Islam to Christianity; that while coaching Muslim children free of charge he would criticise Islam; that he claimed he could prove from the Qur'an that "illicit intercourse, drinking and sodomy are justified in Islam"; that he had prepared a list of various chapters and verses in the Qur'an and marked and underlined those passages in a Qur'an; and finally that he had abused Islam and Muhammad. This accusation was typical of denunciations made on the basis of Pakistan's blasphemy law: a broad range of charges including apostasy, blasphemy, desecration of the Qur'an and insulting Islam and Muhammad, all of which are seen by most Muslims as manifestations of *kufr*, and all of which potentially carry the death penalty in shari'a. The police actually limited their charge to desecration of the Qur'an under Section 295-B.

The accused also offered coaching to children, for which he charged a fee. The accusation apparently originated in Sabir's personal grudge against Iqbal for undercutting his business by offering free coaching.

Mullahs openly threatened Iqbal's advocate and declared that they would kill Iqbal if he were released on bail. Local Christians, and Iqbal himself, felt that in these circumstances prison was the safest place for him.

The Christian community tried its best to avoid publicity for the case, as it feared arousing the mullahs to more aggressive action. The secular media and the Pakistan Human Rights Commission broadcast the news, however, which was then taken up by the international media. The publicity and the efforts made by Western Christian groups to mobilise help for Iqbal were interpreted by many Muslims as a campaign against Islam.

In March 1992 Peerzada 'Ali Ahmed Sabir submitted an application to Additional Sessions Judge Sabah Mohuddin that Tahir Iqbal be sentenced to death for apostasy. The judge heard this new case on 23 April 1992 and dismissed the application, saying that the accused could be sentenced to death only if the prosecution could prove that he had defiled the name of Muhammad.

Tahir Iqbal died in prison on the night of 19-20 July 1992. There was no post mortem, but some Christians suspected that he had been murdered.

Ashiq (Kingri) Masih[174]

Kingri Masih is a Pakistani Christian from Saeedabad who converted to Islam and then reverted to Christianity and attended church with his Christian neighbours. On 17 March 2000 he had an argument with a neighbour, a Muslim religious leader associated with Lashkar-e-Taiba, about his re-conversion. Following this altercation, a mob of 200 men attacked the small Christian community in Saeedabad. On 2 May 2000 the neighbour brought charges against Masih under Section 295-C of the Penal Code for injuring his religious feelings as a Muslim, denying Islam and making derogatory remarks about Muhammad.

The complaint was referred to the District Commissioner for perusal, and then passed on to the police, who registered the complaint. Masih was arrested and refused bail. He denied the allegations.

On 29 June 2002, the death sentence was passed by the Additional District and Session Judge Ch. Mohamad Rafiq in the Faisalabad District and Sessions Court. Masih was also fined 50,000 rupees. His lawyers intended to appeal against the sentence. At the time of writing he is believed still to be in prison.

AFGHANISTAN

Abdul Rahman

Abdul Rahman is an ethnic Pashtun who converted to Christianity in 1990 while working for a Christian non-governmental aid group providing medical assistance to Afghan refugees in Peshawar, Pakistan.

He left for Germany in 1993 and unsuccessfully applied for asylum in Belgium. He returned to Afghanistan after the fall of the Taliban regime in 2001. Abdul Rahman was divorced by his wife for his conversion to Christianity. In the ensuing custody battle over the couple's two daughters his wife and her family raised the issue of his religion as grounds for denying him custody and denounced him to the police in February 2006. He was arrested but refused to renounce his faith, despite the threat of execution. An apostasy charge was laid against him. Although the new Afghan constitution provides for freedom of religion, it limits this by stating that no law can be contrary to shari'a.[175] The prosecutor demanded the death penalty.

The authorities were put under significant pressure by the West to drop the case, but they could not do so easily because of the strength of Islam in the country. They first considered defining Rahman as insane: since the mentally unstable are not liable to the death penalty under the shari'a law of apostasy, the case could then be dropped. Both Rahman himself and the prosecutor opposed this step. Public outrage in Afghanistan increased, and Muslim clerics led violent demonstrations demanding Rahman's execution.

In March 2006 the court (under pressure from the Afghan government) said that there were "investigative gaps" in the case, and Rahman was freed from prison. On 29 March Rahman was offered asylum in Italy, and he lives there now in a secret location.[176]

MALAYSIA

Lina Joy

Lina Joy, a resident of Kuala Lumpur, is an ethnic Malay (her original name was Azlina binti Jailani) who converted from Islam to Christianity in 1998. Since then she has been unable to have her religious status officially changed. As a result of her conversion she suffered imprisonment in a drug rehabilitation centre for men, where on one occasion she was caned on her back in an effort to force her to return to Islam. In addition she was disowned by her family and forced to quit her job. She went into hiding in 2005 because of death threats. A Muslim lawyer who supported her case also received death threats after a poster was released and circulated calling for him to be killed.[177]

Lina Joy began her legal battle to change her official status in 2000 in a civil court. She tried to avoid having the matter handled by a Syariah court (which would have prohibited her from officially leaving Islam), arguing that Article 11 of the constitution guarantees the right of all citizens of Malaysia to choose their own religion. A lower court, however, ruled that civil law could not have precedence over Syariah law in this case. In 2006 Lina Joy appealed to the Federal Court, which is the highest court in Malaysia, but in May 2007 the Court rejected her appeal. A three-judge panel ruled (by two to one) that only the Syariah Court could allow Lina Joy to remove the word "Islam" from her identity card. Malaysia's Chief Justice Ahmad Fairuz Sheikh Abdul Halim said that the panel endorsed legal precedents giving Islamic Syariah courts jurisdiction over cases involving Muslims who want to convert.[178]

The only channel now left for Lina Joy to pursue her claim is the Syariah Court, which can allow her to convert only by declaring her to be an apostate. While she is still registered as a Muslim she is unable to marry her Christian fiancé, because Muslims are forbidden by law to marry outside Islam.

2. Converts from Islam to Christianity in the West

Converts from Islam to Christianity in the West worry constantly about their personal safety. While for most the gravest danger comes from their own families, they are also at risk from Islamic radicals within the Muslim communities in the West. Death threats, violence and harassment are common, and most converts have to move to secret, safe locations and maintain a low profile for fear of being discovered by their persecutors. At the same time they face apathy and misunderstanding from media and authorities that do not represent their cause fairly and do not defend them and their rights. Many Muslims who converted to Christianity in their home countries and then emigrated to the West seeking religious freedom have instead encountered immigration authorities who do not accept that apostasy from Islam presents a threat to their lives in Muslim countries and attempt to deport them back home. In addition the loss of family and community support can involve the loss of their livelihood. If they are immigrants and unable to maintain themselves financially, they can be forced to return to their home countries and face a death sentence there.[179]

UNITED KINGDOM

Many non-Muslims who convert to Islam in Britain are publicly celebrated and applauded. They feel secure and under no threat, able to pursue their lives and careers and proselytise for their new faith. Among such converts are Cat Stevens, Jemima Khan, and the sons of Frank Dobson, the former Health Secretary, and of Lord Birt, the former BBC Director-General.

However, the growing numbers of British Muslims who convert to Christianity may face persecution, and many live in fear. They are likely to be shunned by their family and community, and may also suffer harassment, violent attacks and even kidnapping. A 2007 Policy Exchange study found that 36 per cent of British Muslims aged between 16 and 24 believed that those who converted to another religion should be punished by death, although there are no confirmed reports of converts from Islam being murdered in the UK.[180] Some observers argue that in Western countries with large Muslim populations, Muslims feel under pressure from the majority culture, and the demand to maintain a Muslim identity is intensified: "When identities are precarious, their enforcement will take an aggressive form."[181]

There is no evidence that converts are persecuted by the UK authorities, who will usually try to protect them. However, some victims accuse the police, religious authorities and politicians of finding the issue of apostasy so sensitive that they are reluctant to respond to appeals for help.

The Hussein family[182]

Nissar Hussein is a hospital nurse in Bradford. Born a Muslim, he converted to Christianity in 1996, and his wife converted soon after. Since their conversion they and their children have been regularly jostled, abused, attacked, told loudly to move out of the area and given death threats in the street. His wife has been held hostage inside their home for two hours by a mob. His car, walls and windows have been daubed in graffiti: "Christian b___". Bricks have been thrown through their sitting room window and through their car window. Hussein's car has also been rammed and torched, and the steps to his home have been strewn with rubbish. Recently he was told that his house would be burnt down if he did not repent and return to Islam.

He reported this threat to the police, who told him that such threats were rarely carried out and that he should "stop being a crusader and move to another place". A few days later the unoccupied house next door was set on fire.

Hussein told *The Times*: "It's been absolutely appalling. This is England – where I was born and raised. You would never imagine Christians would suffer in such a way … We feel completely isolated, utterly helpless. I have been utterly failed by the authorities. If it was white racists attacking an Asian guy, there would be an absolute outcry ... They are trying to ethnically cleanse me out of my home. I feel I have to make a stand as an Asian Christian."

"Hannah Shah"[183]

"Hannah Shah", the daughter of an imam in a tightly-knit Muslim community in the north of England, became a Christian after she ran away from home in 1992 (when she was 16 years old) to escape an arranged marriage to a man in Pakistan. In 1994, in fear of her life, she was living in a supposed "safe" house in the middle of a city when her father led a 40-strong mob armed with knives, hammers and axes to find and kill her. They beat on the door, and the imam shouted abuse and death threats through the letterbox, while Hannah cowered upstairs to escape detection. She had to move house 45 times to stay safe from her family.

USA

Paul, an Egyptian convert to Christianity living in Chicago, reported that once his apostasy became known in the local Muslim community he was threatened by radical Muslims who frequented the restaurant at which he worked. As a result he became the target of a sustained campaign of threats and intimidation.[184]

The Washington Times reported that Kris Tedford, a Farsi speaking pastor in Oakton, Virginia, had told them that he had met people who had travelled from Iran to the United States to persecute their relatives who had converted and attempt to bring them back to Islam. If they did not succeed they would attempt to kill the converts.[185]

3. Muslim Intellectuals Deviating
from Orthodox Interpretations of Islam

EGYPT

Naguib Mahfouz[186]

Naguib Mahfouz is the most famous Egyptian literary figure of modern times, a Nobel Prize Laureate in literature (1988). He is an avowed secularist and socialist, and his writings are controversial in Egypt because they address political, social, moral and cultural aspects of Egyptian life. While he claims to be a Muslim, Islamists denounce him as an immoral atheist and Marxist.

His novel *Awlad Haritna* (*Children of our Quarter*), written as an allegory of human history following the main Biblical prophets and dealing with issues of social justice, exploitation and the abuse of power, especially angered radical Islamist fundamentalists, who claimed that he had attacked the dignity of God and distorted the Qur'an, thus becoming an apostate. In October 1994 he was stabbed in the neck by an Islamic extremist outside his home. He was rushed to hospital, and his life was saved. The news of this attack sent shock waves all over the Muslim world, as it signified the growing power of Islamic fundamentalists and their increasing willingness to use physical violence to intimidate those who venture to disagree with them. While many liberals, academics and journalists rallied to Mahfouz's defence and condemned the attack, fundamentalists were emboldened to brand all who disagreed with them as enemies of Islam and apostates.

Following the attempt on his life, Mahfouz has disavowed his secularism, presumably out of fear of Islamic radicals.

Nasr Hamid Abu-Zayd[187]

On 14 June 1995 the Appeals Court in Cairo, Egypt ruled that Dr Nasr Hamid Abu-Zayd, a professor of Islamic and Arabic Studies at Cairo University, was an apostate from Islam and ordered his separation from his wife, Dr Ibtihal Yunis, an assistant Professor of French at Cairo University. The Supreme Court later upheld this decision. Professor Abu-Zayd was consequently denied promotion at the University, and following death threats he fled Egypt with his wife. He now lives in self-imposed exile in Belgium.

Abu-Zayd is a liberal-secularist academic who extended his linguistic research to the study of Islamic source texts, in particular the Qur'an and *hadith*, a step that enraged Islamists. Following his application for promotion at the university on 9 May 1992, he submitted some of his publications to the University Tenure and Promotion Committee. While some members of the committee gave positive reports, Dr 'Abd al-Sabur Shahin, a fundamentalist member of the Committee, wrote a negative report that was cited by the University as the basis for refusing the promotion.

While liberal academics and writers rallied to Abu-Zayd's defence against what they saw as the university's capitulation to radical Islamic pressure, Islamist groups and Al-Azhar University defended the decision on the grounds that secular-liberal ideas and tinkering with the Qur'an and *sunna*[188] texts were unacceptable in an Islamic society. Islamist radicals declared that he had blasphemed against Islam and called for his death.

Muhammad Samida 'Abd al Samad, a former vice-president of the Council of State and a practising lawyer, together with six of his colleagues, brought a legal case against Abu-Zayd on 10 June 1993 seeking his separation from his wife on grounds of apostasy. He was charged with publishing books that "according to reputable scholars" amounted to *kufr*. He was also accused of maligning the Qur'an and *sunna*, Muhammad's Companions and the leading jurists. The Giza Court rejected the apostasy lawsuit in January 1994 on procedural grounds as well as on the ground that no third party has a right to bring about separation between husband and wife. The lawyers appealed against the ruling, and on 14 June 1995 the Cairo Appeals Court reversed the earlier decision and ruled that Abu-Zayd was an apostate, ordering his separation from his wife. It based its ruling on the Islamic principle of *hisba*, which permits any Muslim to defend Islamic morals and behaviour.

The ruling against Abu-Zayd emboldened Islamists to file *hisba* lawsuits against other intellectuals, including Naguib Mahfouz (see above), seeking to separate them from their wives on the ground of apostasy. A new weapon had been added to the Islamists' armoury in their fight against liberals and secularists.

The Supreme Court finally upheld the Appeals Court decision on 5 August 1996, accepting the allegation that Abu-Zayd had described the throne of God, angels, *jinni*, paradise and hell and other teachings of the Qur'an as myths. He had described the Qur'an itself as a cultural product, denied its pre-existence on a tablet in heaven and called it "a linguistic text". Abu-Zayd had also described Islamic Qur'anic sciences as a reactionary heritage, denied the authenticity of the *sunna* and called for emancipation from the authority of religious texts. On these grounds he was accused of *kufr*.

This ruling was the first in modern Egypt in which courts had ruled on the separation of a man from his wife on the ground of apostasy, even though the accused declared that he was a Muslim, and it had far-reaching legal and political implications. It encouraged Islamic radicals to think that they were free to kill Abu-Zayd. The threat of similar accusations served further to quieten liberal intellectuals and severely to limit the exercise of free speech.

Nawwal al-Sa'adawi[189]

The world-famous Egyptian feminist writer, Nawwal al-Sa'adawi, appeared before a Personal Status Court in Cairo in June 2001 to face a private complaint made against her. Sa'adawi was accused of apostasy for comments she had made on religious issues in the Egyptian weekly *al-Midan*. She had allegedly said that the *hajj* pilgrimage to Mecca was a vestige of a pagan practice and had demanded the abolition of Muslim inheritance laws that favour males.

The conservative lawyer Nabil al-Wahsh brought the charge of apostasy against her and demanded that she be divorced from her husband, Sherif. Sa'adawi denied the accusation that she had insulted Islam. This case too was based on the Islamic concept of *hisba*, which allows an individual to sue on behalf of the community. If Sa'adawi had been found guilty, she would have been forcibly divorced from her husband of 37 years and would have faced a three-year prison term.

On 30 July 2001 the Cairo Family Affairs Tribunal dismissed the complaint and ruled that no individual had the right to bring such a case. Sa'adawi welcomed the dismissal as a victory for free thought and expression, saying that she had refused to yield to the mentality of the Dark Ages.

PAKISTAN

Muhammad Younus Shaikh[190]

Muhammad Younus Shaikh, a medical doctor and lecturer at the Homeopathic Medical College in Islamabad, is a devout Muslim interested in reforming Islam to make it relevant to modern contexts. He is founder of "The Enlightenment" organisation, which is committed to propagating democracy and tolerance.

In October 2000, in a discussion in a class he led and in response to a student's question, Shaikh said that Muhammad did not become a Muslim until the age of 40, when he received his first revelation, and that his parents had not been Muslims. Some students reported the matter to local mullahs, and one mullah, affiliated to the extremist organization Majlis Tahaffuz Khatm-e-Nubuwwat, then filed a criminal complaint with the police accusing Shaikh of blasphemy. Shaikh was arrested on 4 October 2000 by the police and held in solitary confinement.

Shaikh's trial was held in closed session inside the Central Jail in Rawalpindi for fear of attacks by Islamist extremists. His solicitors were harassed and threatened with charges of apostasy. Shaikh denied the charge: he declared that his words had been misunderstood and twisted and that he had not said anything blasphemous. Lower Court Judge Safdar Hussain Malik said that Shaikh deserved to be hanged for making derogatory remarks about Muhammad. He was sentenced to death for blasphemy by the Islamabad Additional District and Sessions Court on 18 August 2001, as well as being fined 1,000,000 rupees.

In a letter to the famous Pakistani scholar, Akbar S. Ahmed, asking for his help, Shaikh stated that the blasphemy law was wide open to abuse, especially by mullahs manipulating it for vindictive purposes. He said that a wave of aggressive ignorance, incivility and intolerance was engulfing Pakistan. He stated that the court had found no case against him but that it had succumbed to threats made by militant mullahs, especially by the extremist Aalmi Majlis Khatme-Nabowat Pakistan organisation.

Lawyers working for Shaikh lodged an appeal against the judgment on 21 August 2001, and the Lahore High Court admitted the appeal. On 16 January 2002 the High Court at Rawalpindi rejected his bail application. Some observers said that this decision was intended to protect Shaikh's life from angry radicals.

After Shaikh had spent 15 months in solitary confinement, his case was brought to retrial. No lawyer was willing to defend him, so he had to defend himself using legal books that were smuggled into his cell. The judge at his retrial accepted that his accusers had lied under oath, and he was freed on 21 November 2003. He fled Pakistan and was granted asylum in Switzerland after a *fatwa* was issued calling for him to be killed.

IRAN

Abdollah Nouri[191]

Abdollah Nouri, a high ranking Muslim cleric (*Hojatolislam*), former vice-President of Iran and former Minister of the Interior, aide to President Khatami, and a popular reform-minded politician, was accused on a total of 20 vaguely worded charges, including insulting Islam and being an apostate. He was charged in relation to articles published in his now banned newspaper *Khordad*. On 11 November 1999 the Special Court for the Clergy prevented Nouri from completing his defence and gave him ten days to submit a written text of the defence. On 17 November, however, the Court found him guilty of 15 of the 20 charges (including the publishing of sacrilegious articles, opposing the teachings of Khomeini, insulting Islamic sanctities, undermining the authority of the Supreme Guide, spreading lies and propaganda against the system, insulting the country's religious leadership and supporting renewed ties with the US). It sentenced him to a five-year jail term and banned him from political activity for the same period. It also fined him 15 million Riyals (about US$1,500).

Abdollah Nouri did not appeal against the sentence, stating that he did not recognise the jurisdiction of the Special Court for the Clergy or its verdict. He was jailed in Evin prison. Abdollah Nouri was later granted a pardon by Iran's Supreme Guide, Ayatollah Khamenei, and was released from prison on 5 November 2002.

Hassan Youssef Eshkevari[192]

Hassan Youssef Eshkevari, a *Hojatolislam* (cleric), religious scholar and researcher, was arrested on 5 August 2000 and charged with apostasy, blasphemy, heresy, being at war with God and "corruption on earth" before the Special Court for the Clergy.

Eshkevari had attended an international conference on the future of Iran in Berlin with several other leading reformist activists. In response to a question following his lecture he stated that in his view veiling and the enforcement of a strict dress code for women originated in Iran for cultural and historical reasons and were not required by Islam. Islamic principles relating to social issues were open to change, as Muhammad had sanctioned them only for the needs of his time. These remarks were publicly criticised by conservative clerics in Iran, including the Supreme Guide.

Many other delegates to the Berlin conference were also arrested on their return to Iran and accused of various crimes, which included apostasy, insulting Islam and undermining national security.

The trial was held in closed session, and Eshkevari was denied access to a lawyer of his choice. The court decided on the death penalty. Following domestic and international condemnation, the Head of the Special Court for the Clergy admitted that the trial was flawed. An appeals court overturned the death sentence in May 2001 and sentenced Eshkevari to seven years in prison; it also removed his status as a cleric.

Hashem Aghajari[193]

Hashem Aghajari is a prominent reformist scholar and a history professor at Tabiat-e-Modarres University in Tehran as well as Head of its History Department. He is a member of the political party The Organization for Islamic Mujahidin of the Revolution and an ally of former President Khatami. Aghajari was sentenced to death on 7 November 2002. He had made a speech in June 2002 commemorating the death of 'Ali Shariati, the main ideologue of the Iranian Islamic Revolution. In his speech, he called for a reformation of Islam similar to the Protestant Reformation in Christianity, which would entail a return to the original core of Islam while repudiating various additions adopted over the centuries. He also questioned the hardline interpretations of the ruling clerics, accusing them of setting themselves up as mediators between God and the believers, a status that runs counter to the nature of Islam. Aghajari denied criticising Muhammad in any way and apologised for any unintended offence his remarks may have caused.

Aghajari was arrested, held in solitary confinement in Evin prison and denied legal counsel. On 7 October 2002 he was put on trial behind closed doors before a Hamadan court for apostasy, blasphemy against Muhammad, insulting the Shi'a imams and top state religious authorities and being one of the "corrupt on earth". Judge Ramazani of the Fourteenth District Court in Hamadan handed down a sentence of death and in addition 74 lashes, eight years imprisonment and internal exile and a ten-year prohibition from teaching. Iranian courts frequently issue multiple sentences in cases where they want to set an example. Should the death penalty be implemented, the other punishments will obviously not be carried out. His lawyer said there would be an appeal.

Experts claim that Aghajari's arrest and prosecution were part of an overall clampdown on freedom of expression in Iran. The case was also seen by many as another instance of the hardliners, led by Ayatollah Khamenei, trying to intimidate President Khatami and his reformist allies.

University students publicly protested against the verdict, claiming it was an insult to the university community and a violation of freedom of speech. They chanted slogans against Mahmoud Hashemi Shahroudi, the hardline chief of Iran's judiciary. Sensing the growing mood of antagonism to the hardline policies of his followers, Supreme Guide Khamenei ordered a review of the case. At the end of a retrial, Aghajari was again condemned to death. President Mohammad Khatami spoke up on his behalf, saying that he had done more for Iran than the "inexperienced" judge who sentenced him. The Supreme Court again overturned his conviction. Finally, in July 2004, he was convicted of the lesser offences of insulting sacred Islamic tenets. The court sentenced him to three years imprisonment, and a further two years suspended.

Aghajari was finally released in July 2004, emerging from Evin prison in north Tehran to a warm welcome by relatives and friends after two years of legal battles with judges and mass demonstrations by students.[194]

BANGLADESH

Taslima Nasrin[195]

Taslima Nasrin, a doctor turned writer and women's rights activist, was subjected to threats in October 1993 from the militant Islamist movement Council of Soldiers of Islam. They called for her death following the publication of her novel *Lajja* (*Shame*), which portrays the experiences of a Hindu family being attacked by Muslims after the destruction of the Babri mosque in India. The group claimed that Nasrin had hurt their religious sensibilities.

In 1994 an Indian newspaper quoted Nasrin as saying the Qur'an should be rewritten. Nasrin claimed that she was misquoted and that she meant that Islamic law should be changed to give women more rights.

A devout Muslim, Zainal Abedin Babul, filed a petition against Nazrin claiming she had insulted Islam and hurt his religious feelings. She was also charged with deliberately and maliciously outraging religious feelings. Islamic militants organised demonstrations demanding her death for blasphemy and issued death threats against her. Police found her at the top of a hit list of Bangladeshi intellectuals drawn up by radicals. Following the issue of an arrest warrant, Nasrin fled Bangladesh for Sweden and later New York.

Nasrin returned to Bangladesh briefly in September 1998 to be with her mother, who later died of cancer. She had to remain in hiding, appearing only for a court hearing, after which she was granted bail on the 1993 charges of insulting religion. She then went into exile abroad again.

MUSLIM INTELLECTUALS IN THE WEST

Salman Rushdie[196]

This case has received so much publicity that it will be mentioned only very briefly. In 1981 Salman Rushdie published his novel *The Satanic Verses*, which provoked outrage among Muslims worldwide. In 1989 Ayatollah Khomeini of Iran issued a *fatwa* calling for the death of Rushdie for blasphemy and for insulting Islam and Muhammad. Rushdie was forced to go into hiding until 1998, when the Iranian government stated that it would not track down the writer nor carry out the death sentence. There are however, continued calls for the *fatwa* to be implemented, and ten years after the original *fatwa* was issued, several Iranian clerics continued to justify it and call for Rushdie's death. Typical is Grand Ayatollah Makarem Shirazi, who is reputed to have said: "Anyone who blasphemes the Prophet or all that is sacred in Islam is condemned for apostasy. Anyone who sees this book [*The Satanic Verses*] has to admit that Rushdie committed the highest form of blasphemy to the Prophet".[197] In 2009, the twentieth anniversary of the *fatwa*, a group of Iranian lawmakers, political activists, and analysts said that they considered the fatwa "irrevocable".

Ayyan Hirsi Ali

Ayyan Hirsi Ali, a Somali political scientist in the Netherlands, had to go into hiding in 2002 after receiving a barrage of hate mail and death threats from Muslims. This followed a live debate on Dutch TV in which she accused Islam of treating women shoddily, and conservative Muslim groups of covering up cases of domestic violence and child abuse. Hirsi Ali also condemned the government's support for programs promoting multiculturalism, which (she claimed) help to keep Muslim women isolated from Dutch society. She claimed that Islam was facing backwards because of its treatment of women. Following her receipt of explicit death threats, the police told her to move house, and the mayor of Amsterdam provided bodyguards. Finally she decided to leave the Netherlands in October 2002.[198]

Khalid Duran[199]

Khalid Duran is a well known liberal Muslim scholar who was born in Germany and moved to the US in 1980, where he taught at Temple University and American University. He is also editor of the journal *TransIslam*. Recently he published a book, *Children of Abraham: An Introduction to Islam for Jews* (Jersey City, NJ: Ktav Publishing House, 2001).

An edict against Duran – not a full *fatwa* – was issued by Sheikh Abdul Moneim Abu Zant, an Islamic cleric in Jordan and a leader in the Islamic Action Front, the political arm of the Muslim Brotherhood. This was reported in the Jordanian Weekly *Al-Shahed*, which is close to the Jordanian Muslim Brotherhood, in its 6 June 2001 issue. Sheikh Abdel Moneim Abu Zant found the book offensive to Islam and issued a religious opinion declaring Duran an apostate, advocating his death by stating that "his blood is permissible", and calling on Muslims in the United States to "unify against him". He also urged two prominent Sunni Islamic institutions to issue similar judgments of apostasy against Duran. In Islamic religious terms such declarations mean that any Muslim who kills the accused is fulfilling a religious duty.

As a result Duran, at the age of 61, moved from his home in the Washington suburbs to a safe house and was provided with 24-hour private security. He stated that he had received death threats over the years for some of his writings criticising extremist Islamic groups, but that this was the first time he had become the target of a religious edict concerning apostasy.

4. Sectarian Groups Within Islam

THE BAHA'IS (IRAN)

The Baha'i faith was founded in the 19th century in Iran as an off-shoot of Twelve Shi'ism. It came to be seen as heretical by the orthodox establishment. As a result, Baha'is in Iran have experienced cycles of persecution. Granted a respite under the last Shah, who treated them well, they prospered until the 1979 Islamic Revolution. The clerical ruling elite was virulently hostile to the Baha'i faith as a heresy which had to be blotted out, and the Baha'i community has been severely persecuted ever since. In the first six years following the revolution over 200 Baha'is, mainly community leaders, were executed. Baha'i institutions have been disbanded, their property confiscated, their holy places and cemeteries desecrated. Baha'is cannot hold government jobs, enforce legal contracts, practise law, collect pensions, attend universities or practise their faith. They have been deprived of all civil rights.

Zabibullah Mahrami

Zabibullah Mahrami was a mid-ranking civil servant in the Department of Agriculture of the Provincial Government of Yazd, Iran. Soon after the revolution he publicly renounced his Baha'i faith, following the Shi'a doctrine of *taqiyya*, which permits dissimulation in times of danger and persecution. His adoption of Twelver Shi'a Islam was reported in the newspapers at the time. Many other Baha'is made similar pronouncements in order to protect themselves from persecution, stay out of trouble and keep their jobs, as many Baha'is were dismissed from state employment and had their pension rights suspended.

After a few years of lying low, Mahrami judged that revolutionary zeal had abated and began to visit Baha'i meetings and participate in Baha'i festivals. In August 1995 he was charged with apostasy in the Yazd Revolutionary Court. Mahrami admitted that he had converted to orthodox Shi'a Islam because he had been afraid for his own safety and that of his family, and that when he thought that Baha'is would no longer be harassed, he reverted to his Baha'i faith.

Following shari'a guidelines for dealing with apostates, the court first tried to guide Mahrami back to Islam. When he refused, he was charged with apostasy and with insulting Islam, and on 2 January 1996 the court declared him guilty of these charges and sentenced him to death.

While the constitution of the Islamic Republic of Iran does not mention apostasy in its penal code, the court cited a legal exegesis of Ayatollah Khomeini as the basis for its decision. The verdict was passed on to the Supreme Court for approval, but it ruled that the Revolutionary Court was not the appropriate tribunal for this kind of case and referred the case to a Civil Court.

The authorities, however, did not comply with the Supreme Court ruling. Instead they brought new charges of espionage on behalf of Israel against Mahrami in a Revolutionary Court. In February 1997 the court sentenced him to death for spying.[200]

THE AHMADIS (PAKISTAN)

The Ahmadis are a Muslim revivalist movement founded by Ghulam Ahmad of Qadian (Punjab) in the 19th century. Although they consider themselves to be true Muslims, the majority Sunni population of Pakistan, as well as the Shi'a minority, have always viewed them as heretical for claiming that their founder was the promised Mahdi and had a prophetic role. Since the movement's foundation there have been many calls by orthodox Muslim groups for its suppression by state legislation and by the state enforcement agencies. Pakistani governments gradually yielded to the demands of Islamic extremists, who also instigated violent riots against Ahmadis, and in 1974 a constitutional amendment was introduced by the then Prime Minister Zulfikar Ali Bhutto declaring Ahmadis to be a non-Muslim minority. In April 1984 President Zia-ul-Haq promulgated sections 298-B and 298-C of the Pakistan Penal Code, which made it a criminal offence for Ahmadis to call themselves Muslims, to employ Muslim terms and appellations associated with Islam, to use Muslim worship practices or to propagate their faith. As a result Ahmadis have been subjected to a wide range of abuses, based mainly on the blasphemy laws, which have been used to harass, intimidate and detain them.[201]

Mirza Mubarak Ahmad Nusrat[202]

Mirza Mubarak Ahmad Nusrat, an Ahmadi of Mirpurkhas, Pakistan, was arrested in 1989 for allegedly distributing "prayer pamphlets" (*mubahila*) and was detained in the police cells. A Sunni opponent, Mullah Ahmad Mian Hamadi, visited the police station to enquire about the progress of the case and was infuriated to see Nusrat praying as a Muslim (according to Pakistani law Ahmadis must not "pretend" to be Muslims). He brought a charge against Nusrat, and a criminal case was registered against him at Tando Adam police station under section 298 of the Pakistan Penal Code for posing as a Muslim and offending the feelings of Muslims.

Nusrat was kept in jail for eleven years while his case was heard in various places: Tando Adam, Sanghar, Hyderabad and Karachi. The accused and his advocate, Ali Ahmad Tariq, had to travel thousands of miles for the various court appearances. The case was referred to the Sindh High Court on three occasions, and finally that court ordered it to be transferred to Hyderabad. On 20 May 2000 the judicial magistrate of Hyderabad, Fida Hassan Mughal, convicted Nusrat for an offence under section 298 of the Penal Code for offering prayers like a Muslim (facing Mecca and prostrating himself). The judge took into account the eleven years the accused had already spent in jail and sentenced him to "only" two months and 21 days' imprisonment.

Nasir Ahmad[203]

Nasir Ahmad, an Ahmadi of Nankana in the District of Sheikhupura, issued invitation cards for his daughter's wedding, which was scheduled for 15 May 1992. The card carried the normal greetings for such occasions, including phrases like "In the Name of God, the Gracious, the Merciful", "We Invoke Praise and Blessings on the Noble Prophet", "May Peace be Upon You", and "Inshallah". A radical mullah of the local Khatm-e-Nubuwwat Association brought a charge against 13 members of the family, accusing them of blasphemy and of offending the feelings of Muslims. Two of the accused were women and one was a nine-month-old baby. The police sought advice from their legal department, which based its decision on a precedent from the Lahore High Court and directed the police station to register a criminal case.

Nasir Ahmad remained in prison for three months, until released on bail. The judicial process lasted three years. First the Lahore High Court decided that a charge could be brought under section 295-C. Then the case went before the Supreme Court, where the Additional

Advocate General, Farooq Haider, claimed that the state had reached the limit of its patience in tolerating "these people" (Ahmadis). The Supreme Court decided that section 295-C was not applicable to the case but that other sections of the Penal Code were.

Finally, on 23 April 1995, the Additional Sessions Judge in Sheikhpura sentenced Ahmad to four years' imprisonment under section 295-A of the Code and to two years imprisonment under section 298-C.

5. Non-Muslims Perceived as Insulting Islam

Michel Houellebecq

In September 2002 Michel Houellebecq, a French philosopher, was taken to court by the Paris Mosque and the World Islamic League for incitement to racial hatred. In one of his novels he had depicted a woman being killed by Islamic terrorists. He had also described the Qur'an as appalling. The court cleared him of all charges on 22 October 2002, agreeing that his remarks were a judgment on a religion, not an incitement to hatred.[204]

Oriana Fallaci[205]

In June 2002 legal proceedings were started in France by a coalition of Islamic and anti-racism groups (including the Movement Against Racism and for Friendship Between People) against the Italian author Oriana Fallaci, a well known Italian journalist, for her book *La Rabbia e L'Orgoglio* (*Rage and Pride*), which warned of an Islamist menace to Western civilisation and freedoms and accepted the concept of a clash of cultures and of religions between Islam and the West. Muslims accused her of Islamophobia and xenophobia. On 20 June 2002 the Geneva-based Islamic Centre also filed a suit against her, in Switzerland under Swiss anti-racism laws, and asked for her book to be banned. Fallaci died in 2006.

Sir Vidia Naipaul

Sir Vidia Naipaul was much criticised by British and US Muslim leaders, and called a reactionary and an Islamophobe, for his book *Beyond Belief: Islamic Excursions Among the Converted Peoples* (NY: Random House, 1998), in which he stated that Islam was an Arabic religion and that all non-Arab Muslims were converts robbed of their original identity and cut off from their authentic roots by Islam. In a lecture in 2002 he compared Islam with colonialism, again claiming that it destroyed its adherents' history and identity. Following threats to his life, his wife Nadira Khanum Alvi, herself a Muslim, wrote to a Pakistani newspaper in his defence.[206]

Conclusion

The above discussion illustrates the interpenetration of Muslim political and religious identities and the serious view taken by many Muslims of the rejection of Islam by a Muslim. This attitude results from the way in which Islamic sources and history have been interpreted by jurists and scholars and implemented by rulers from the beginning. Despite differences and minority opinions there is broad agreement in Islamic law, both Sunni and Shi'a, about the basic penalties for apostasy, including the execution of adult male apostates.[207] Shari'a *hudud* and *ta'zir* laws against apostasy, blasphemy and unbelief, all of which potentially carry the death penalty, are the basis for their attacks.

This book has sought to describe the great variety of measures used in Muslim societies and states against any deviation from whatever form of Islam is normative in each place. In some countries the state legal system has adopted shari'a laws that enable official charges to be made within the state courts against converts from Islam. (These blasphemy and apostasy laws enable the state arbitrarily to detain citizens who for any reason are viewed with disfavour by the authorities or by militant Muslims.) In these contexts self-appointed guardians of "true" Islam may level accusations of apostasy, blasphemy, heresy, desecration of the Qur'an and insulting Islam or Muhammad. Many specific accusations result from personal grudges borne by the accusers against the defendants; others are brought by militant Islamic organisations intent on purifying Muslim societies from any hint of deviation, heresy, innovation and reform.

Where such provisions do not yet exist, or where state legal systems are not interested in such prosecutions, groups and individuals within the society may act instead to carry out what they see as obligatory shari'a penalties. Islamic scholars and mullahs may issue private *fatwas* demanding the killing of the accused, and families may use coercive measures, which sometimes culminate in murder, as they try to expunge the shame that they feel conversion brings on the whole family. In some contexts mobs can be easily incited to frenzied attacks against an alleged apostate.[208] Individual Muslims zealous for their religion and its honour may take it on themselves to assassinate the accused, believing that they are doing a holy service to God and to Islam.

The law of apostasy in Islam stands in stark contrast to modern understandings of human rights and religious liberty. According to Article 18 of the United Nations Universal Declaration of Human Rights, "Everyone has the right to freedom of thought, conscience and religion; this right includes the freedom to change his religion or belief." This freedom to change one's religion is completely denied in Islam. The reviewed cases highlight the negative impact of the Islamic attitudes to apostasy and blasphemy on freedom of expression and treatment of minorities. Given the rise in Islamist power across the Muslim world and the increased application of shari'a in new regions and states, such travesties of justice are likely only to increase.

Muslims are well aware that the rest of the world finds their apostasy law outrageous, and they sense themselves to be under attack from the liberal West and accused of contravening universally accepted, individual human rights. But apostasy continues to be considered a shocking and repulsive crime by most Muslims. They therefore tend instinctively to justify the strict shari'a penalties as commensurate with the severity of the act, which (they believe) is committed against the very basis of the Muslim nation (*umma*) and amounts to deliberate treason, betrayal of the Islamic cause, and an attack on Islam itself and its honour. Some more liberally minded scholars and others raise their voices bravely in dissent, but the threat of the application of the apostasy and blasphemy laws against any who criticise them is used efficiently to intimidate opponents, silence criticism, punish rivals, reject innovations and reform and keep non-Muslim communities in their place. The Muslim voices calling for reform of the law represent only a small proportion of the world's Muslims.

The only hope for real freedom of religion within Islam lies in the abolition of all penalties for apostasy and permission for those who want to leave Islam to do so.

Appendix 1:
Apostasy: Major and Minor

Yusuf Al-Qaradawi, 13 April 2006
www.islamalive.net/English/contemporary/2006/04/article01c.shtml
(viewed 1 July 2009)

Yusuf Al-Qaradawi (1926-) is a very prominent and popular Egyptian cleric and scholar based in Qatar and is alleged to be the Muslim Brotherhood's spiritual leader. Qaradawi is the most influential Sunni cleric in the Muslim world today. He has helped set up numerous global Islamic institutions and was behind the founding of the Al Jazeera TV channel. He is President of the International Union of Muslim Scholars and of the European Fatwa Council. He has his own Arabic-language website and supervises the popular site Islam Online. He has written over 100 books on Islam.

Facing Apostasy: The Role of Muslims

The greatest kind of danger that faces Muslims is that which threatens their moral aspect of existence, i.e., their belief. That is why apostasy from Islam is regarded as one of the most dangerous threats to the Muslim community. The ugliest intrigue the enemies of Islam have plotted against Islam has been to try to lure its followers away from it; they have even used force for this purpose.

In this regard, Almighty Allah says, [**And they will not cease from fighting against you till they have made you renegades from your religion, if they can.**] (Al-Baqarah 2:217)

In the contemporary age, the Muslim community has been exposed to horrendous invasions and aggressive attacks, one of which is the missionary invasion that aims at uprooting the Muslim community altogether. This invasion began its missions with the Western colonialism (of the Muslim world), and it still exercises its activities in the Muslim world and among the Muslim communities and minorities (in non-Muslim countries). One of its goals is to entice Muslims to convert to Christianity. This goal was made clear in the North American Conference on Muslim Evangelization (that was held in Colorado in 1978). Forty studies about Islam and Muslims and how to spread Christianity among them were submitted to that conference, and US$1 billion was allocated for this purpose. In addition, the Zwemer Institute (in South Carolina) was established to train missionaries to preach Christianity to Muslims.

Another example is the communist invasion that spread through many Muslim countries in Asia and Europe and made every effort to put an end to Islam and grow generations who know nothing about Islam at all.

The third and most dangerous and cunning kind is the secular invasion, which still plays its role in the Muslim world, sometimes openly, and sometimes in disguise. It seeks to undermine true Islam and approves of the superstitious manifestations that are falsely claimed to belong to Islam.

The duty of the Muslim community — in order to preserve its identity — is to combat apostasy in all its forms and wherefrom it comes, giving it no chance to pervade in the Muslim world.

That was what Abu Bakr and the Prophet's Companions (may Allah be pleased with them) did when they fought against the apostates who followed Musailemah the Liar, Sijah, and Al-Aswad Al-'Ansi, who falsely claimed to be Allah's prophets after the demise of Prophet Muhammad (peace and blessings be upon him). Those apostates had been about to nip the Islamic call in the bud.

It is extremely dangerous to see apostasy prevailing in the Muslim community without facing it. A contemporary scholar described the apostasy prevailing in this age saying, "What an apostasy; yet no Abu Bakr is there to (deal with) it."[1]

Muslims are to seriously resist individual apostasy before it seriously intensifies and develops into a collective one.

That is why the Muslim jurists are unanimous that apostates must be punished, yet they differ as to determining the kind of punishment to be inflicted upon them. The majority of them, including the four main schools of jurisprudence (Hanafi, Maliki, Shafi'i, and Hanbali) as well as the other four schools of jurisprudence (the four Shiite schools of Az-Zaidiyyah, Al-Ithna-'ashriyyah, Al-Ja'fariyyah, and Az-Zaheriyyah) agree that apostates must be executed.

In this regard, many hadiths were reported in different wordings on the authority of a number of Companions, such as Ibn 'Abbas, Abu Musa, Mu'adh, 'Ali, 'Uthman, Ibn Mas'ud, 'A'ishah, Anas, Abu Hurairah, and Mu'awiyah ibn Haidah.

For example, Ibn 'Abbas quoted the Prophet (peace and blessings be upon him) as having said, "**Whoever changes his religion, then kill him.**"

A similar wording of the hadith was reported on the authority of Abu Hurairah and Mu'awiyah ibn Haidah with a sound chain of transmission. Also, Ibn Mas'ud reported the Prophet (peace and blessings be upon him) as having said, "**The blood of a Muslim who testifies that there is no god but Allah and that I am the Messenger of Allah is not lawful to shed unless he be one of three: a married adulterer, someone killed in retaliation for killing another, or someone who abandons his religion and the Muslim community.**"

Another version of this hadith was reported by 'Uthman, "**The blood of a Muslim is not lawful to shed unless he be one of three, a person that turned apostate after (embracing) Islam or committed adultery after having married, or killed a person without just cause.**"

The eminent scholar Ibn Rajab said, "Punishing a person by death for committing any of these sins is agreed upon among Muslims."[2]

'Ali ibn Abi Talib (may Allah be pleased with him) punished some people who apostatized from Islam and claimed that he was a god by putting them to fire after having reprimanded them and asked them to return to Islam but to no avail. He put them to fire saying these following lines of poetry:

When I saw the matter so flagrant,
I kindled fire and summoned for Qanbar"
Qanbar was the servant of Imam 'Ali.[3]

Ibn 'Abbas did not agree with 'Ali about burning the apostates, quoting, as evidence for his opinion, the Prophet's hadith, "**Do not punish anybody with Allah's punishment (of fire).**" According to Ibn 'Abbas, the apostates should have been killed by a means other than burning. Thus, Ibn 'Abbas was not against killing the apostates in principle, but against killing them by fire.

Abu Musa and Mu'adh also punished a Jew by death, as he had embraced Islam and then reverted back to Judaism. Mu'adh said about that: "It is the verdict of Allah and His Messenger."

'Abdur-Raziq also reported, "Ibn Mas'ud held in custody some Iraqi people who had apostatized from Islam, and then wrote to Caliph 'Umar asking him what to do with them. 'Umar wrote him back, saying, 'Ask them to return to the true religion (of Islam) and the Testimony of Faith. If they are to accept this, set them free, and if they are to reject it, then kill them.' When Ibn Mas'ud did so, some of the apostates repented and some refused, and thus, he set free the repentant and killed those who renounced Islam after being believers."[4]

It is also reported on the authority of Abu 'Umar Ash-Shaybani that when Al-Mustawrad Al-'Ajli converted to Christianity after having embraced Islam, 'Utbah ibn Farqad sent him to 'Ali, who asked him to return to Islam, but he refused, and thus 'Ali killed him.[5]

Major and Minor Apostasy

Ibn Taymiyah mentioned that the Prophet (peace and blessings be upon him) accepted the repentance of a group of apostates, and he ordered that another group of apostates, who had committed other harmful acts to Islam and the Muslims, be killed.

For instance, on the day of the conquest (*fath*) of Makkah, the Prophet (peace and blessings be upon him) ordered that Maqis ibn Subabah be killed, as he had not only apostatized from Islam but also insulted and killed a Muslim person. He (peace and blessings be upon him) also ordered that Ibn Abi Sarh be killed, as he had apostatized from Islam and also sought to spread falsehood and slander.

> The Prophet (PBUH) accepted the repentance of a group of apostates...

In this respect, Ibn Taymiyah differentiated between two kinds of apostasy, an apostasy which does not cause harm to the Muslim society and an apostasy in which apostates wage war against Allah and His Messenger and spread mischief in the land. The repentance of the apostates in the first kind is accepted; while in the second kind, it is not if it occurs after the apostates have fallen into the power of the Muslim authority.[6]

'Abdur-Raziq, Al-Baihaqi, and Ibn Hazm reported that Anas returned from a mission for jihad and went to 'Umar, who asked him, "What has been done with the six people from (the tribe) of Bakr ibn Wa'il who have apostatized from Islam?" Anas said, "O Commander of the Believers, they are people who turned apos-

> **Ibn Taymiyah differentiated between the harmful apostasy and the harmless one.**

tate and joined the polytheists, and thus they were killed in the battle." 'Umar commented, "We belong to Allah and to Him we will return." Anas wondered, "Had their penalty been but death?" 'Umar replied, "Yes. I would have asked them to return to Islam, and had they refused, I would have imprisoned them."[7]

This attitude of 'Umar was also held by Ibrahim An-Nakh'I, and Ath-Thawri, who said, "This is the viewpoint that we follow."[8] Ath-Thawri also said, "The punishment of the apostate is to be deferred so long as there is a hope that he may return to Islam."[9]

In my point of view, as the scholars have differentiated between major and minor innovations in religion and between mere innovators and those who spread and call for their innovations in religion, we can also differentiate between major and minor apostasy, and between apostates who do not wage war against Islam and Muslims and those who proclaim their apostasy and call for it.

Major apostasy, which the apostate proclaims and openly calls for in speech or writing, is to be, with all the more reason, severely punished by the death penalty, according to the majority of scholars and the apparent meaning of the Prophet's hadiths. Otherwise, An-Nakh'i and Ath-Thawri's view which was built on 'Umar's attitude may be followed.

Apostates who call for apostasy from Islam have not only become disbelievers in Islam but have also become enemies of Islam and the Muslim nation. They, by doing so, fall under the category of those who wage war against Almighty Allah and His Messenger and spread mischief in the land.

According to Ibn Taymiyah, waging war against something may be done by already attacking it or by speaking against it. The latter may be far more dangerous than the former with regard to religions. So is also the case with spreading mischief: it may be through causing physical damage or through causing moral harm, and the latter is, likewise, far more hazardous than the former with regard to religions. This proves how much more harmful it is to wage war against Allah and His Messenger by speaking against them and seeking to spread mischief in the land.[10]

In Arab culture, we say that the pen is mightier than the tongue. Writing about something may be far more effective than merely speaking about it, especially in this day and age, as writings can be widely published.

On another hand, the apostate is deprived of its love, loyalty, and cooperation according to Almighty Allah's words, [**And he amongst you that turns to them (for friendship) is of them**] (Al-Ma'idah 5:51). This far exceeds the punishment of execution in the view of the people of common sense.

Why Is Apostasy Severely Punished in Islam?

The Muslim community is based on belief and faith. Belief is the basic foundation of its identity, pivot, and spirit of its life. That is why it does not allow anyone to harm this identity. Hence, proclaiming apostasy is considered the most flagrant crime in the eyes of Islam as it poses a danger to the identity of the Muslim community and its moral being. In other words, it jeopardizes the first five main objectives of the Shari'ah, which Islam with its moral and legislative systems seeks to preserve — religion, life, offspring, the intellect, and property. Religion occupies the very first place here as believers may sacrifice themselves, their country, and their wealth for the sake of their religion.

Islam does not compel people to join it nor does it force anybody to accept or to leave any other religion, but it places great importance upon conviction for those who embrace it. Almighty Allah says, [**Had your Lord willed, all the people on earth would have believed. So can you (Prophet) compel people to believe?**] (Yunus 10:99)

He Almighty also says, [**Let there be no compulsion in religion: truth stands out clear from error.**] (Al-Baqarah 2:256)

Almighty Allah does not accept that religion be taken lightly...

However, Almighty Allah does not accept that religion be taken lightly: a person joining it one day and forsaking it another day, in the like manner of the group of Jews about whom the Qur'an says, [**A section of the People of the Book say: believe in the morning what is revealed to the believers, but reject it at the end of the day; perchance they may (themselves) turn back.**] (Aal 'Imran 3:72)

Besides, Islam does not call for the execution of apostates who do not proclaim their apostasy or call for it. Rather, it leaves the punishment for the hereafter if they die in the state of apostasy, as Almighty Allah says, [**And if any of you turn back from their faith and die in unbelief, their works will bear no fruit in this life and in the hereafter; they will be companions of the fire and will abide therein.**] (Al-Baqarah 2:217). However, this type of apostate may receive a discretionary punishment in this world.

> **Islam does not call for the execution of apostates who do not proclaim their apostasy or call for it.**

The death penalty with regard to apostasy is to be applied only to those who proclaim their apostasy and call for others to do the same. Islam lays down this severe punishment in order to protect its unity and the identity of its community. Every community in this world has basic foundations that are to be kept inviolable, such as identity, loyalty, and allegiance.

> **Apostasy involves a change of loyalty and identity...**

Accordingly, no community accepts that a member thereof changes its identity or turns his or her loyalty to its enemies. They consider betrayal of one's country a serious crime, and no one has ever called for giving people a right to change their loyalty from a country to another whenever they like.

Apostasy is not only an intellectual situation whose handling is confined to discussing the principle of freedom of belief; it also involves a change of loyalty and identity. People who apostatize from Islam give up their loyalty to the Muslim nation and pay allegiance, heart and soul, to its enemies. This is denoted in the agreed-upon hadith that clarifies the kinds of people whose blood is lawful to shed and describes among those people the apostate, by saying, "**Or someone who abandons his religion and the Muslim community**" (Ibn Mas'ud).

The phrase, "And the Muslim community," is part of the description of an apostate; this entails that every apostate from Islam by implication abandons the Muslim community.

Although apostasy is a criminal act, apostates' rights are not to be violated, nor are they punished except for the things they do or proclaim, verbally or in writing (against Islam and the Muslims); as speaking or acting against Islam openly is a clear-cut disbelief and cannot be interpreted otherwise. Should there be any doubt in this regard, the person accused of apostasy would be given the benefit of the doubt.

Negligence in punishing apostates who proclaim and call for their apostasy jeopardizes the whole community and exposes it to afflictions whose consequences Almighty Allah only knows. This may lead to apostates' enticing other people, especially the gullible and those of weak faith, to join them. This, in turn, may lead to those apostates forming a group hostile to the Muslim nation and seeking the help of its enemies against it. In this way, the Muslim nation will fall into intellectual, social, and political disputes and disintegration, which may develop into bloody ones or even into a civil war that could destroy everything.

One scenario took place in Afghanistan when a group of people gave up their religion and adopted communist beliefs after they had studied in Russia. They were recruited by the Communist party. The Afghani people were heedless of this danger, which gave the chance for this group to hold power in Afghanistan; and by virtue of their authority, they set to wholly change the identity of the Muslim community there. But the Muslim Afghans did not give in; they resisted as much as they could and formed the valiant Afghani jihad against the communist apostates, who even dared to request Russian military help against their people and country. The Russian troops attacked Afghanistan with tanks and artillery and heavily bombarded it.

That was the scenario of the ten-year-long civil war that destroyed Afghanistan and caused the death and injury of millions of people there.

All that was a result of ignoring the issue of the apostates and remaining silent about their crime of apostasy from the beginning. Had those renegades been punished before the situation became serious, the Afghani people would have been saved from the evils of this aggressive war and its destructive results.

Ideological Guidelines

I would like to lay down the following guidelines that are relevant to judging apostates:

1. Judging whether someone has apostatized from his or her religion is a very serious matter that entails being deprived of his or her family and community. When a married man apostatizes from Islam, he is separated from his wife and children, as it is not lawful for a Muslim woman to be married to a disbeliever;[11] and with regard to children, he is no longer trusted to take care of them. In addition, there is a material punishment to be inflicted upon him, according to the scholarly consensus. Hence, all kinds of certainty must be established when judging a person — who has been certainly known to be a Muslim — as an apostate. Mere doubt here is to be disregarded altogether. One of the most horrendous things which the Prophet's Sunnah seriously warned against is to label someone disbeliever without having any legal proof to say so.

2. Issuing fatwas about the apostasy of a certain person is within the competence of reputable scholars who are well-versed in Islamic jurisprudence and can differentiate between clear-cut evidences and those which are ambiguous, between the verses whose meanings are established and those whose meanings are allegorical, and between religious texts wherefrom possible deductions may be made and those which must be taken literally. They are not to label someone an apostate unless there is no alternative but to do so, such as (making sure that) he or she has denied a fundamentally established principle of religion or mocked at it, or insulted Almighty Allah and His Messenger publicly, verbally or in writing, and the like.

The gravity and seriousness of the issue of passing judgment in this regard dictates that it is not left at any rate to the discretion of unqualified scholars, who may give hasty and groundless judgments in this respect.

3. It is the Muslim ruler who should carry out the punishment of the apostate. The punishment should be decided according to the judgment of the Muslim judiciary. This judgment should be based only on Almighty Allah's Law, which derives its rulings from the evidences in Allah's Book and the Sunnah of His Messenger, as the Qur'an and Sunnah are the main sources to which people are to resort when they differ on something. Almighty Allah says in this respect, [If ye have a dispute concerning any matter, refer it to Allah and the Messenger if ye are (in truth) believers in Allah and the Last Day] (An-Nisaa' 4:59).

The qualification for being a competent judge in Islam requires that one possess knowledge of the rulings of Shari'ah by way of personal reasoning (*ijtihad*) from primary religious texts. And if a person lacks this qualification, he or she must seek the help of reputable scholars who are capable of *ijtihad*, so that they can uncover the truth and not issue groundless judgments or pass them out of whims, in which case he would be doomed to Hellfire (on the Day of Judgment).

4. The majority of scholars are of the opinion that apostates should be asked to repent and return to Islam before punishment is inflicted upon them. Moreover, Ibn Taymiyah, in his book, *As-Sarim Al-Maslul 'ala Shatim Ar-Rasul*, wrote, "The Prophet's Companions (may Allah be pleased with them) were unanimous that the apostate be asked to repent and return to Islam before punishment is inflicted upon him."

Some jurists say that an apostate should be given a 3 day respite to repent; some say it is less than this, some say it is more, and some others say he is to be asked for this for as long as he lives. Some scholars, however, made exception of the hypocrite (*zendiq*), who pretends to be a Muslim never actually was. According to certain scholars, repentance cannot be accepted from hypocrites. This applies also to those who insult the Prophet (peace and blessings be upon him).

The purpose of the respite given to apostates here is to give them a chance to review their situation, as they may overcome their state of confusion and become convinced of Islam as the true religion; if they are really seekers of the truth. But if their apostasy is based on desires or an activity in the interest of the enemies of Islam, may Almighty Allah severely punish them.

Some contemporary intellectuals say that it is Almighty Allah, not man, who accepts (or refuses) repentance. But this has to do with the rulings of the hereafter. As with those of this world, the apparent repentance (of sinners), and declaring their Islam, is to be accepted by the concerned authorities. Almighty Allah orders us to judge people according to their apparent states, and their intentions are up to Him to decide upon. In this regard, an authentic hadith is reported to the effect that the blood and property of those who bear witness that there is no god but Allah will be inviolable and that their reckoning will be with Allah (concerning their intentions and what they harbor in their hearts).

Therefore, if individuals were to take it upon themselves to label people as apostates and judge them accordingly as deserving the death penalty, and, moreover, seek to implement the penalty themselves, it would pose a great danger to people's lives and properties. If this were to happen, it would entail that ordinary unqualified people would possess three authorities simultaneously: the authority of giving fatwas — by accusing certain people of being apostates — the authority of passing judgments, and the authority of carrying out those judgments. In other words, they would be acting as muftis, prosecutors, judges, and police all together.

Refuting Objection of Intellectuals

Some contemporary writers who are not versed in religious knowledge object to the penalty of proclaimed apostasy being death by saying that this penalty is not mentioned in the Qur'an. It is only mentioned in a hadith *ahad* (hadith that is narrated by people whose number does not reach that of the *mutawatir*, which is hadith that is narrated by such a large number of people that they cannot be expected to agree upon a lie, all of them together); and hadiths *ahad*, according to them, are not taken as evidences for the legal punishments prescribed by Shari'ah.

But this objection is refutable in many aspects as follows. First, according to the scholarly consensus, the authentic Sunnah is a source for applied rulings in Shari'ah. Almighty Allah says, [**Say: Obey Allah and obey the Messenger.**] (An-Nur 24:54). He also says, [**Whoso obeyeth the Messenger obeyeth Allah.**] (An-Nisaa' 4:80)

As for the hadiths specifying the death penalty for apostates, they have been proven to be authentic. Besides, they were put into effect by the Companions in the era of the Rightly-Guided Caliphs.

In addition, claiming that hadiths *ahad* are not taken as evidences for the legally prescribed punishments is not tenable, as all the followed schools of jurisprudence have depended in prescribing the penalty for alcohol consumption on the hadiths *ahad* reporting the punishment thereof. However, the hadiths *ahad* which were reported about the penalty of apostasy are greater in number and more authentic than those reported about the punishment of alcohol consumption.

Had it been true that hadiths *ahad* were not to be applicable with regard to the legally prescribed penalties, this would have led to disregarding the Sunnah as the second primary source of Shari'ah right after the Qur'an, or at least disregarding 95 percent (if not 99 percent) thereof. This, in turn, would have also undermined the principle of abiding by Allah Almighty's Qur'an and the Sunnah of His Prophet. This is because, scholarly speaking, hadiths *ahad* constitute the majority of the hadiths tackling the rulings of Shari'ah; and *mutawatir* hadiths, which are analogous to *ahad* ones, are of such rarity that some eminent scholars of Hadith, as mentioned by Ibn As-Salah in his distinguished introduction of the sciences of Hadith, said that they are hardly found.

Many of the writers denying hadiths *ahad* as a source of the rulings of Shari'ah do not know what exactly hadiths *ahad* refer to. They think that they are those reported only by one transmitter of Hadith, which is wrong, as hadiths *ahad* are those related by groups of individuals fewer than those said to have related *mutawatir* hadiths at one or more stages of the transmission of the hadiths, though traced through contiguous, successive narrators back to the Prophet (peace and blessings be upon him). An *ahad* hadith may have been reported by two, three, four, or more Companions and still a multiple number of successors reported it on their authority.

In this respect, the hadith referring to inflicting the death penalty upon apostates was reported by a large number of the Companions, some of whom were referred to above. Hence, it is a clear well-known hadith in this respect.

Second, another considerable source of Shari'ah in Islam is scholarly consensus (on the rulings thereof). With regard to apostasy, all Muslim jurists of all schools of jurisprudence, Sunni and Shiite, agree that apostates must be punished. And most jurists, furthermore, agree, with the exception of 'Umar, An-Nakh'i, and Ath-Thawri, that their punishment is death. Nevertheless, there is scholarly consensus that apostasy is considered a punishable crime.

Third, some early Muslim scholars are of the opinion that the following verse refers to how to deal with apostates, [**The punishment of those who wage war against Allah and His Messenger, and strive with might and main for mischief through the land is: execution**] (Al-Ma'idah 5:33). Of those scholars are Abu Qulabah and others.[12]

We have referred to Ibn Taymiyah's opinion to the effect that waging war against Allah and His Messenger by speaking openly against them is more dangerous to Islam than physically attacking its followers and that moral mischief in the land is more hazardous than physical mischief.

This is further supported by the fact that among the hadiths that say that the blood of a Muslim is not lawful to shed unless he be one of three persons, there is a hadith reported on the authority of 'A'ishah to the same effect, but instead of saying, "**Someone who abandons his religion and the Muslim community,**" she reported, "**Or someone who goes out waging war against Allah and His Messenger, in which case he is to be killed, crucified, or expelled from the land.**" This proves that the immediately above-mentioned verse includes reference to the apostates.

Note also that Almighty Allah says, [**O ye who believe! Whoso of you becometh a renegade from his religion, (know that in his stead) Allah will bring a people whom He loveth and who love Him, humble toward believers, stern toward disbelievers, striving in the way of Allah, and fearing not the blame of any blamer. Such is the grace of Allah which He giveth unto whom He will. Allah is All-Embracing, All-Knowing.**] (Al-Ma'idah 5:54)

This verse indicates that Almighty Allah has prepared a group of believers, whose characteristics are referred to in the verse, to deal with apostates, by being "**stern toward disbelievers,**" as was the case with Abu Bakr and the believing Companions with him when they protected Islam against apostasy.

There are also a number of verses about the hypocrites indicating that they protected themselves against being killed because of their disbelief by way of making false oaths to the contrary to flatter the believers. Among these verses are the following, [**They have made their oaths a screen (for their misdeeds)**] (Al-Mujadilah 58:16); [**They will swear unto you that ye may be pleased with them**] (At-Tawbah 9:96); and [**They swear by Allah that they said nothing (wrong), yet they did say** the word of disbelief] (At-Tawbah 9:74).

According to these verses, the hypocrites denied their disbelief and swore to it, which indicates also that had there been clear proofs of their disbelief, their false oaths would not have protected them from being punished.[13]

Apostasy of Rulers

The most dangerous kind of apostasy is that of rulers, whom are supposed to protect the Muslim nation's beliefs, resist apostasy, and uproot apostates altogether from the Muslim community. However, we find that many rulers welcome apostasy secretly and openly; proclaim dissoluteness flagrantly and in disguise; and protect apostates and confer titles and decorations upon them.

These kinds of rulers favor Allah's enemies and are against Allah's true worshippers. They take religious beliefs lightly, belittle Shari'ah, disrespect divine and prophetic ordinances and prohibitions, and disdain the sacred emblems and symbols of the Muslim nation, namely, the members of the Prophet's household, his pious Companions, the Rightly-Guided Caliphs, the eminent religious scholars, and the heroes of Islam.

Moreover, they consider adhering to the ordinances of Islam, such as the performing of prayers in mosques for men and the wearing of veils for women, a crime and a manifestation of extremism. Not only this, but they also seek to proclaim and apply the philosophy of "undermining the sources" (from which the true Muslims derive the right courses to follow) in the educational process, the media, and the culture, so as to hinder the construction of a true Muslim mentality. Furthermore, they pursue the true callers for Islam and obstruct every faithful call and movement that aims at reviving religion and upgrading this world on its basis.

However, it is strange that this kind of people, in spite of their flagrant apostasy, are interested in preserving the outward appearance of Islam, so that they cunningly use it in demolishing Islam; the Muslim nation thus treats them as Muslims, yet they seek to undermine its basic internal structure (of belief). They may even seek to have a connection with religion by encouraging false manifestations of religion and bringing close to them insincere religious scholars who flatter them and who are described by some as "the scholars of the (political) authority and agents of the police."

The situation is thus complicated, for if those people hold in their power the official bodies responsible for issuing fatwas and the judiciary, who may judge them as apostates or punish them for their open disbelief? The Prophet (peace and blessings be upon him) referred to the open disbelief of this kind of people in a hadith that states the following:

> 'Ubadah ibn As-Samit said, "We gave the Prophet the pledge of allegiance for Islam, and among the conditions on which he took the pledge from us, was that we were ... not to fight against the ruler unless we noticed him having open kufr (disbelief), for which we would have a proof with us from Allah." (Al-Bukhari and Muslim)[14].

Here comes the role of the Muslim public opinion that is to be led by the reputable scholars and people who call people to Islam and unbiased intellectuals. Should it be hindered from exercising its role, its abhorring resistance will certainly lead someday to putting an end to those oppressive apostates; for it is not easy for the Muslim community to lose its identity or make concessions with regard to its beliefs and message.

French colonialism in Algeria and Russian colonialism in Muslim majority countries fiercely tried to uproot Muslim identity therein, although they had no effect. Colonialism and tyranny came to an end, while Islam and the Muslims remained. However, the war waged against Islam on the part of some secularist rulers of some Muslim countries, as well as some secularist Muslim immigrants, is proved to be fiercer and more dangerous than that which colonial powers waged against Islam and Muslims.

Hidden Apostasy

There is another kind of apostasy among people who do not declare their explicit disbelief and openly wage war against everything that is religious. Those apostates are far smarter than that. They wrap their apostasy in various coverings, sneaking in a very cunning manner into the mind, the same way that malignant tumors sneak into the body. These people are not noticed when they invade or begin to disseminate their falsehood, but they are mostly felt when they affect the minds. They do not use guns in their attacks; however, their attacks are fierce and cunning.

Reputable scholars and well-versed jurists are aware of this type of apostates, but they cannot take action in the face of such professional criminals, who have firmly established themselves and have not left a chance for law to be enforced on them. They are the hypocrites whose abode will be in the lowest level of Hellfire.

This is intellectual apostasy, whose traces are noticed everyday in circulated newspapers and books, in radio and TV programs, and in laws legislated to govern people's affairs. This kind of apostasy is — at least in my point of view — more dangerous than openly announced apostasy; for the former works continuously on a wide scale, at the same time, it cannot be easily resisted in the same manner as the latter, which always makes much fuss, attracts attention, and stirs up public opinion.

Hypocrisy is more dangerous than open disbelief. This fact will be clearly discerned when one reflects back to the great danger which the leader of Madinah's hypocrites, 'Abdullah ibn Ubayy, posed to Islam. The Madinah's hypocrites were more threatening to Islam than Abu Jahl and the pagans of Makkah. It is for this that the Qur'an specified only two verses for dispraising disbelievers at the beginning of Surat Al-Baqarah, while hypocrites were given a share of thirteen verses in the same surah.

Intellectual apostasy is continuously propagated night and day. We feel its relentless and ruthless effects on our society. It needs a wide-scale attack at the same level of power and thought. The positive religious obligation here is for Muslims to launch war against such a hidden enemy; to fight it with the same weapon it uses in waging attacks against the society. Here comes the role of reputable scholars who are well-versed in Islamic Jurisprudence.

It is true that the pioneers of this new form of apostasy are well supported on the media level, but the power of truth, the faith reposed in the hearts of believers, and Allah's support are more than enough to vanquish this falsehood and pierce the hearts of those who spread it with their own daggers. Here, we will feel joyful with this Divine victory and will really understand the following verse, [**Nay, We hurl the truth against falsehood, and it knocks out its brain, and behold, falsehood doth perish! Ah! Woe be to you for the (false) things ye ascribe (to Us)**] (Al-Anbiyaa' 21:18).

In conclusion, we have nothing to say but to recite the verse that reads, [**Thus doth Allah (by parables) show forth truth and vanity. For the scum disappears like forth cast out; while that which is for the good of mankind remains on the earth. Thus doth Allah set forth parables**]

(Ar-Ra'd 13:17).

Notes

1   Title of a treatise by the eminent scholar Abu Al-Hasan An-Nadawi.

2   Majama' *Az-Zawa'id*, vol. 6, p. 261.

3   See the interpretation of "the fourteenth hadith" in *Jami' Al-'Ulum wa Al-Hikam*. Revised by Shu'aib Al-Arna'ut. (Dar As-Salam ed).

4   See *Nail Al-Awtar*, vol. 8, p. 506, (Dar Al-Jil ed).

5   Reported by 'Abdur-Raziq in his *Musannaf*, vol. 10, p. 168. saying no. 18707.

6   *Ibid*, saying no. 18710.

7   Ibn Taymiyah, *As-Sarim Al-Maslul*, p. 368 (As-Sa'adah ed, verified by Muhey Ad-Din 'Abdul-Hamid).

8   'Abdur-Raziq, *Al-Musanaf*, vol. 10, pp. 165-166, saying no. 18696; Al-Baihaqi, *As-Sunan*, vol. 8, p. 207; Sa'id ibn Mansur, p.3, saying no. 2573; Ibn Hazm, *Al-Muhalla*, vol. 11, p. 221 (Al-Imam ed). This attitude of 'Umar indicates that he did not see the death penalty as a regular punishment for apostasy to be applied in each case a person apostatizes from Islam; it might be cancelled or deferred if there was a necessity for this. The necessity in the accident quoted was the state of war and the close distance between those apostates and the disbelievers, which may expose the former to temptation and confusion by the latter. 'Umar might have based his judgment on holding analogy between this case and the one in which the Prophet (peace and blessings be upon him) was reported to have said, "Hands (of thieves) are not to be cut off during wartime;" this was for fear that the thief whose hand would be cut might get so distressed that he would join the enemy.

There might be another reason for 'Umar's judgment in that situation. He might have believed that when the Prophet (peace and blessings be upon him) said, "Whoever changes his religion, then kill him" as a leader of the Muslim nation. In other words, it was a decision of the executive authority and a matter of political legislation, not a revelation from Allah. Accordingly, putting the apostate to death is not a binding ruling to be followed in every case. Rather, it is a decision for those in authority in the government to take; if it orders that the apostate be executed, it must be put into effect, and vise versa. This is similar to what the Hanafis and Malikis derived from the hadith that reads, "He (the soldier) who kills an enemy will take the possessions of this enemy;" and to what the Hanafis concluded from the hadith that says, "He who reclaims a barren land will have it." See my book, *The General Characteristics of Islam*, p. 217.

9   'Abdur-Raziq, *Al-Musanaf*, vol. 10, saying no. 18697.

10   Ibn Taimiyah, *As-Sarim Al-Maslul*, p. 321.

11   Ibn Taymiyah, *As-Sarim Al-Maslul*, p. 385.

12   The Egyptian judiciary had praiseworthy precedents in separating between spouses on the basis of the apostasy of one of them (having embraced the Bahai faith). There is a verdict issued in this respect by Judge 'Ali 'Ali Mansur; the verdict is published in a special treatise and supported by a verdict issued by the State's Tribunal on 11/7/1952. The verdict reads, "The rulings pertaining to apostasy [in Shari'ah] must be wholly applied even though the current penal law does not stipulate the capital punishment unto the apostates. Let the apostate (who converted to the Bahai faith) bear the responsibility (for his deeds) at least by annulling his marriage, so long as there are judiciary bodies in the state that have judicial authority by virtue of the court's direct or collateral capacity."

13   Al-Hanbali, Ibn Rajab, *Jami' Al-'Ulum wa Al-Hikam*, p.320.

14   Ibn Taymiyah, *As-Sarim Al-Maslul*, pp. 346-347.

Appendix 2:
Freedom of Religion in Islam

M.A. Zaki Badawi, unpublished paper presented 10 January 2003

The late Zaki Badawi (1922–2006), was a prominent Egyptian Islamic scholar who was appointed the first chief imam at London's Regent's Park Mosque and Cultural Centre in 1978. In 1986 he established the Muslim College in London, of which he became President. Badawi was elected chairman of the Imams and Mosques Council by the National Conference of Imams and Mosque Officials of the UK in 1984. He was considered to be the dean of Muslim scholars in Britain and the unofficial leader of Britain's Muslims for many years. Considered a moderate and a reformer, he supported interfaith dialogue and was awarded the KBE in 2004. He was a co-founder of the Three Faiths Forum, vice chairman of the World Congress of Faiths and director/trustee of the Forum Against Islamophobia and Racism (FAIR).

Article 18 of the Universal Declaration of Human Rights (UDHR) presented Muslim countries with a serious challenge. The Declaration itself assumes that the member states of the United Nations are secular in the sense that religion is not the dimension that determines citizenship. This is in contrast to the mediaeval system in which the membership of a particular faith, and even a specific interpretation of it, forms the basis for legitimate membership of the state. People with doubtful loyalty were subjected to the Inquisition in Europe and to the Mihnah (ordeal) in Baghdad.

Although all Muslim countries are more or less secular in their political structure, and most of them have adopted Western legal systems rather than the Shariah (Muslim Law), nevertheless there are aspects of the Shariah that remain in force in most of them.

Islamic family law is followed by all Muslim countries, with the exception of Turkey and possibly Tunisia. The question of freedom of expression, conscience and belief is addressed sympathetically in most constitutions but is often violated. The dethronement of the Shariah from the official state legal system of the Muslim states stifled its development to deal with the changing world and social conditions. With the wide spread clamour for the return to the Shariah and the attachment of the population to its precepts, governments have had to pay heed to public opinion and refer issues such as freedom of religion to the religious authorities. The Muslim scholars normally follow one or the other of the Islamic Schools of Law (Madhahis – singular: Madhab). The prevailing schools are four Sunni: Hanafi, Maliki, Shafi'i and Hanbali. The Shi'i schools are the Imami and Zaidi. The Kharijite School is the Ebadi. These Schools of Law came into being as a result of the work of eminent jurists interpreting Muslim Law as enshrined in the Qur'an and the Tradition of the Prophet. The story of religious freedom in Islam begins therefore from the time of the Prophet.

The Qur'an and the Prophetic Traditions: General Principles and Early Application

The Qur'an contains numerous verses emphasizing freedom of religion: for example "Remind [them of the Unity of God] for you are only a reminder. You have no control over them." Sura 88 verses 21-22). A clearer declaration occurs in Surah 2 verse 265 "There shall be no coercion in matters of faith." Alongside these and similar verses, the Tradition tells us that the Prophet in Madina where he established the first Muslim authority (622 C.E.) signed an agreement with the Jews of the city granting them full rights of citizenship and complete freedom to uphold their beliefs and perform their acts of worship and follow their customs undisturbed.

The Wars of the Prophet

The career of the Prophet involved him in conflict primarily with the polytheistic Arab tribes, and especially with his own tribe of Quraish of Mecca. There was a period of truce between the Prophet and the tribal Arabs, which was broken by the latter. The Muslims mounted an attack on Mecca itself and conquered it in 630 C.E. thus destroying the centre of resistance to Islam. The Qur'an records some of the campaigns and the directives given to the Prophet with regard to their aims. The ninth Sura of the Qur'an begins with a declaration of ending the peaceful coexistence between the Muslims that "once the sacred months are over slay the polytheists wherever you may come upon them." The other polytheistic tribes were forced into Islam as the Muslims were instructed in Surah 9 verse 5 "Once the sacred months are over slay the polytheists wherever you may come upon them" Thus the campaigns ended with victory for the Prophet and the final suppression of the Arab traditional religion.

Relationship with the Jews

The relationships with the Jews soured and they joined the opposition to the Prophet. Consequently they lost their position as equal citizens and were made to pay Jizia (head tax) Sura 9 verse 29. The 29th verse of the same Sura states, "Fight those who have been given scripture but do not believe in God and the Day of Judgement ... until they pay the tribute".

The Prophet is also reported as saying "I have been instructed to fight the people until they say There is no God but Allah." This militant attitude is regarded by some as the last and final statement of Islam, regarding other faiths. They view Islam to be in a perpetual state of war against other religions claiming that those verses calling for peaceful preaching of the faith have been abrogated, as they were only relevant to the period of Muslim weakness and impotence. Others believe that the wars of the Prophet were defensive in nature and that persuasion was his means to conversion. The dispute over this is reflected in the views of the scholars at a later age as will be shown below. Notwithstanding the above, we know that the Prophet did not suppress Judaism or Christianity and he is reported to have instructed that the <u>dualist</u> Zoroastrians should be treated like the Peoples of the Book, i.e. to be granted freedom of religion while their able bodied men should pay Jizia or head tax.

The Period of the Guided Caliphs (632-661 C.E.)

The death of the Prophet and the succession of the first Caliph Abu Bakr occasioned wide spread rebellions in Arabia against the authority of Madina. The rebels were labelled apostates. Abu u Bakr persuaded his colleagues to declare war against these rebels to bring them back to the fold. In simultaneous and well-planned campaigns the rebels were defeated and Arabia was once more unified. The action of Abu Bakr against the 'apostates' together with statements attributed to the Prophet that "whosoever changes his religion is to be killed" formed the foundation of the rule governing apostasy in Islam. The Peoples of the Book, (the Jews, the Christians) and the Zoroastrians, were granted their religious freedom on payment of the Jizia (head tax). The ancient Arab religion continued to be illegitimate and became extinct.

There are reports of the apostasy of individuals and small groups during the life of the Prophet and during the reign of the second Caliph Omar. In all of them, the responsible officials administered the death penalty without allowing for a period to recant. Omar is reported to have disagreed with the decision and said that had he been present he would have given the apostate time to come back to Islam.

The Successive Dynasties

Thirty years after the death of the Prophet the dynastic system of government became the norm in the world of Islam. The rules concerning the freedom of Muslims to change their religion were formulated by scholars in various parts of the Muslim empire. The death penalty was generally accepted for male and female apostates. Ibrahim Al-Nakhi (d. 713 C.E.) opposed the death sentence and suggested that the apostate should be given unlimited time to recant. His opinion, however, was ignored by the founders of the now established Schools of Law.

It must be pointed out, however, that Al-Nakhi disputed the death sentence only and not the principle of coercion. Apparently he found no evidence in the Qur'an for such a severe penalty and did not accept as authentic the Traditions calling for the death sentence. But he, like all the other jurists of the first Islamic century, called for the Istitabah, that is inducing the apostate to recant. The method suggested by the Caliph Omar, according to reports, was imprisonment.

The Hanifi School in the second Islamic century would suggest such treatment for women. They rejected the death penalty for women following the Prophet's instruction not to kill women and they also reasoned that women pose no danger to the state as they do not normally bear arms. Fighting women, therefore, are to be treated like men. This rationale should have led to a different assessment of the

Wars of Apostasy as being war to avert the threat to the stability of the state rather than a war to force people to believe. Generally the jurists regarded apostasy to be a danger to the social order. Since the foundation of the state was religion, apostasy was regarded as a betrayal equal to high treason in a secular system.

As suggested earlier jurists, with a few exceptions, supported the death penalty for the apostate and this remains the case to the present day.

What is apostasy?

The definition of apostasy is crucial to our understanding of the attitude of Muslim jurists to religious freedom.

Abu Bakr's wars were waged against rebels who shared the same basic beliefs. Some were Muslims in conviction but they refused to pay the Zakat (religious tax) to Abu Bakr. They argued that the Qur'an states that the Zakat was paid to the Prophet as purification and so that he would pray for the donors (Surah 9 verse 103) and Abu Bakr has no such status. Abu Bakr dismissed this argument and treated them as apostates. The other uprisings were directed at the dominance of the Quraish, the tribe of the Prophet. Leaders of these tribal revolts claimed to be prophets of equal status to that of the Quraishi prophet. Musailamah the 'prophet' of the Banu Hanifah sought to divide Arabia between his tribe and Quraish. There were also a few cases of individuals converting to other religions. All these instances were listed by historians as cases of apostasy. The jurists came to define apostasy as the renunciation of Islam either through converting to another religion, or becoming an atheist, or rejecting well known parts of the Shariah such as the prohibition on the consumption of wine or treating Islamic texts with disrespect, or insulting God or the Prophet or any of the Prophets mentioned in the Qur'an, or holding an unacceptable doctrine. This rather catchall definition allowed rulers to suppress opposition by labelling its leader an apostate. The doctrine of predestination supported by the Ummayyads, who ruled for close to a century 661-756 C.E. was regarded as a fundamental part of the creed. Consequently those who advocated free will were put to death.

The political use of apostasy continued after the fall of the Ummayyad and the emergence of the second Islamic dynasty, the Abbasids (756-1257 C.E.). There was a rise of Persian nationalism which was led by some of the most brilliant thinkers and poets. The authorities accused them of Zandaqah. The Zindiqs were defined as those who profess Islam while secretly adhering to Zoroastrianism or other ancient Persian religions. It is possible that some Persians did go back to their former faiths but the presence of some of the most illustrious intellectuals leads to the suspicion that the accusation of Zandaqah was politically motivated. To support this interpretation is the fact that the accused were not allowed to recant and their profession of faith was not accepted, and further worse still the guilt was established generally by accusation. The jurists at the time supported these severe measures despite their violations of the Shariah rules that demand proper evidence and suspend punishment on the confession of faith.

Again under the seventh Abbasid Caliph, Al-Ma'mun (813-833 C.E.), the doctrine of the creation of the Qur'an was imposed and those who did not openly accept it were tortured and some were even killed.

Alongside state intolerance of opposition to its doctrine, the public in all Muslim countries have never tolerated those holding views at variance with those commonly held. Many scholars suffered mob persecution, sometimes for minor deviations. Tabari, (d. 923 C.E.) the great historian, exegetist and jurist was declared an apostate by the Hanbalis of Baghdad. His crime was not to recognize the founder of their madhab (school of law) as a jurist. Theologians, philosophers, jurists and Sufis suffered such fate and many books were burned on the altar of their supposed apostasy.

The Modern Age

The conquest of the land of Islam by various European powers occasioned the suspension of the Islamic penal code, though the mob continued to impose its will when the opportunity arose.

Most Muslim states, as mentioned earlier, expressed reservations in connection with Article 18. Apostasy is still punishable by death in countries like Saudia Arabia, Pakistan, Iran and at one time the Sudan. It remains illegal in all the other Muslims countries though not so punishable.

The jurists' legacy in relation to this issue did not simply centre on the punishment; it also decreed that the apostate lose all legal rights as a person. He/she would be deprived of property and lose the status of being married. The property, according to most authorities, goes to the state. Only a minority of jurists allowed relatives to acquire the property of the apostate as if he were dead. So even those who opposed the death sentence supported this loss of legal personality. This has consequences in the present day. In 1986 a university professor in Egypt was declared by the High Court to be an apostate and ordered to be separated from his wife. Professor Nasr Abu Zayd and his wife left Egypt and joined the University of Leiden in the Netherlands.

Many people were puzzled by this judgment because the constitutions of Egypt supports freedom of expression. More confusing still, the professor continued to declare his allegiance to Islam. The ideas that brought about this judgement were not debated with him to show him that he had deviated from the faith. To make matters worse the venerable Al-Azhar authority supported the judgment.

Professor Abu Zayd could have lived in Egypt without being molested by the authorities. A similar judgment against the journalist Sheikh Ali Yousef was passed early in the 20th century. He defied it and continued to live with his wife. What really worried Professor Abu Zayd was the reaction of the mob.

Religious agitators in Egypt by condemning writers, novelists and thinkers, incited assassins to make attempts on their lives. The journalist Faraj Foda was killed. The Nobel Laureate Naguib Mahfouz was knifed, while others have to have 24-hour police protection.

In Pakistan the Blasphemy Law promulgated by General Zia ul-Haq led to thousands of arrests threatened with the death penalty.

The Apostasy Law though only applies to Muslims; the Dhimmi (that is a non-Muslim living in a Muslim state) is bound not to insult the Prophet or Islam. A young Christian boy was imprisoned having been accused of writing insulting remarks on a wall. This despite the fact the child was shown to be illiterate. He was sentenced to death but the Appeal Court released him in 2002.

The followers of Mirza Ghulam Ahmad (d. 1908), the Ahmadis, are persecuted in Pakistan. They believe their leader to have been a prophet confirming the Shariah of the Prophet Muhammad and to be the promised Mahdi and the Messiah. They believe him to have abolished the jihad and therefore reject any punishment for apostasy. In 1974 the Parliament of Pakistan declared the Ahmadis to be non-Muslims. Many Ahmadis lost their government jobs and their places of worship were not to be called mosques. They were denied permission to perform the Hajj (the Pilgrimage to Mecca). Their leader was forced to seek refuge in London where he established his headquarters.

In the Sudan under General Numeiry the religious and political leader Mahmud Muhammad Taha was executed for apostasy (heresy) in 1985 when Numeiry introduced Shariah in the Sudan. Dr. Hassan Al-Turabi, the leader of the Islamic Front and known Islamic reformer, was at the time a member of the government. In a bizarre manifestation of support the Saudi authorities sent a delegation to congratulate the Sudanese on their achievement.

In Iran there is the perennial case of the Bahais, the followers of Mirza Hussain Nur Ali Baha Allah (d. 1892) who founded a new religion and fled Persia in the nineteenth century. Though he himself was an apostate, his followers are born to the creed; but the authorities in Iran before and after the Revolution treat them as apostates. They are subjected to persecution but not executed for being Bahai.

New Interpretation of the Shariah

The Qur'anic declaration that "There shall not be coercion in matters of faith" has been used by apologists to proclaim Islam's commitment to freedom of religion. The apostasy law could not obviously be reconciled with this principle. Attempts were made to square the circle. A prominent contemporary preacher, Muhammad Al-Ghazali, suggested that you are free to follow any religion until you convert to Islam in which you will have consciously signed your freedom away by choice! Obviously, this sophistry cannot apply to those who are born Muslim.

The more meaningful examination of the issue came from the leaders of the reform movement Muhammad Abdu (d. 1905) and his student Rashid Ridha (d. 1936). In their commentary on the Qur'an (Tafseer Al-Manar) they argued that the Qur'an guarantees freedom of religion.

Abdu's other student Mahmud Shaltout, the former Grand Sheikh of Al-Azhar, echoed the views of his teacher in his book "Al Islam 'Akida wa Sharia" publisher Al Shuruq 1992 pp.280-281. But by far the most elaborate and clear statement from a religious authority came from eminent sheikh Abd Al-Muta'al Al-Sa'idi. He published a book in 1955 entitled "Al-Hurriyyah al-Dimiyyah fi al-Islam" Freedom of Religion in Islam. He makes the categorical statement: "the apostate has the right to freedom of religion. This is my Madhab which is new. He should be treated like a person who has never been a Muslim." P.134. This book was republished in the year 2000 in the face of strong opposition from some religious bodies in Al-Azhar and elsewhere. This is an indication of the deteriorating state of religious freedom in the country and in Al-Azhar itself. The quote is from this edition (published by Dar Al-Ma'arif in Cairo 2000). The author being confident of his position included in the second edition of this book the critical articles authored by a prominent Azharite conservative and rebutted his argument.

The reissuing of this book may indicate that there is a serious move in favour of religious freedom in Muslim learned circles.

Contemporary "Islamic Movements" that have been in the forefront of supporters for the death penalty for apostasy are beginning to have second thought. This will involve them in reinterpreting the wars of the Prophet and his Companions and the verses of the Holy Qur'an and the texts of the Tradition. Leading this trend is Shaikh Ghanoushi, the leader of the Al-Nahda Party of Tunisia. He states in his book Al-Hurriayat Al-'Am Fi Al-Daula Al-Islamiyya published by Markaz Dirasat Al-Wahda Al-Arabiyya in 1993 pp. 48-51 that he favours freedom of religion and the apostate should be treated like any other nonbeliever. He cites several modern religious scholars in support of this view in addition.

How long will it take to trickle down to the common people? Only then will sensible debate about some of the most important areas of the Shariah take place in a proper academic atmosphere.

Appendix 3:
Universal Declaration of Human Rights

Adapted and proclaimed by the General Assembly of the United Nations, 10 December 1948

Preamble

Whereas recognition of the inherent dignity and of the equal and inalienable rights of all members of the human family is the foundation of freedom, justice and peace in the world,

Whereas disregard and contempt for human rights have resulted in barbarous acts which have outraged the conscience of mankind, and the advent of a world in which human beings shall enjoy freedom of speech and belief and freedom from fear and want has been proclaimed as the highest aspiration of the common people,

Whereas it is essential, if man is not to be compelled to have recourse, as a last resort, to rebellion against tyranny and oppression, that human rights should be protected by the rule of law,

Whereas it is essential to promote the development of friendly relations between nations,

Whereas the peoples of the United Nations have in the Charter reaffirmed their faith in fundamental human rights, in the dignity and worth of the human person and in the equal rights of men and women and have determined to promote social progress and better standards of life in larger freedom,

Whereas Member States have pledged themselves to achieve, in co-operation with the United Nations, the promotion of universal respect for and observance of human rights and fundamental freedoms,

Whereas a common understanding of these rights and freedoms is of the greatest importance for the full realization of this pledge,

Now, Therefore THE GENERAL ASSEMBLY proclaims THIS UNIVERSAL DECLARATION OF HUMAN RIGHTS as a common standard of achievement for all peoples and all nations, to the end that every individual and every organ of society, keeping this Declaration constantly in mind, shall strive by teaching and education to promote respect for these rights and freedoms and by progressive measures, national and international, to secure their universal and effective recognition and observance, both among the peoples of Member States themselves and among the peoples of territories under their jurisdiction.

Article 1.

All human beings are born free and equal in dignity and rights. They are endowed with reason and conscience and should act towards one another in a spirit of brotherhood.

Article 2.

Everyone is entitled to all the rights and freedoms set forth in this Declaration, without distinction of any kind, such as race, colour, sex, language, religion, political or other opinion, national or social origin, property, birth or other status.

Furthermore, no distinction shall be made on the basis of the political, jurisdictional or international status of the country or territory to which a person belongs, whether it be independent, trust, non-self-governing or under any other limitation of sovereignty.

Article 3.

Everyone has the right to life, liberty and security of person.

Article 4.

No one shall be held in slavery or servitude; slavery and the slave trade shall be prohibited in all their forms.

Article 5.

No one shall be subjected to torture or to cruel, inhuman or degrading treatment or punishment.

Article 6.

Everyone has the right to recognition everywhere as a person before the law.

Article 7.

All are equal before the law and are entitled without any discrimination to equal protection of the law. All are entitled to equal protection against any discrimination in violation of this Declaration and against any incitement to such discrimination.

Article 8.

Everyone has the right to an effective remedy by the competent national tribunals for acts violating the fundamental rights granted him by the constitution or by law.

Article 9.

No one shall be subjected to arbitrary arrest, detention or exile.

Article 10.

Everyone is entitled in full equality to a fair and public hearing by an independent and impartial tribunal, in the determination of his rights and obligations and of any criminal charge against him.

Article 11.

(1) Everyone charged with a penal offence has the right to be presumed innocent until proved guilty according to law in a public trial at which he has had all the guarantees necessary for his defence.

(2) No one shall be held guilty of any penal offence on account of any act or omission which did not constitute a penal offence, under national or international law, at the time when it was committed.

Nor shall a heavier penalty be imposed than the one that was applicable at the time the penal offence was committed.

Article 12.

No one shall be subjected to arbitrary interference with his privacy, family, home or correspondence, nor to attacks upon his honour and reputation. Everyone has the right to the protection of the law against such interference or attacks.

Article 13.

(1) Everyone has the right to freedom of movement and residence within the borders of each state.

(2) Everyone has the right to leave any country, including his own, and to return to his country.

Article 14.

(1) Everyone has the right to seek and to enjoy in other countries asylum from persecution.

(2) This right may not be invoked in the case of prosecutions genuinely arising from non-political crimes or from acts contrary to the purposes and principles of the United Nations.

Article 15.

(1) Everyone has the right to a nationality.

(2) No one shall be arbitrarily deprived of his nationality nor denied the right to change his nationality.

Article 16.

(1) Men and women of full age, without any limitation due to race, nationality or religion, have the right to marry and to found a family. They are entitled to equal rights as to marriage, during marriage and at its dissolution.

(2) Marriage shall be entered into only with the free and full consent of the intending spouses.

(3) The family is the natural and fundamental group unit of society and is entitled to protection by society and the State.

Article 17.

(1) Everyone has the right to own property alone as well as in association with others.

(2) No one shall be arbitrarily deprived of his property.

Article 18.

Everyone has the right to freedom of thought, conscience and religion; this right includes freedom to change his religion or belief, and freedom, either alone or in community with others and in public or private, to manifest his religion or belief in teaching, practice, worship and observance.

Article 19.

Everyone has the right to freedom of opinion and expression; this right includes freedom to hold opinions without interference and to seek, receive and impart information and ideas through any media and regardless of frontiers.

Article 20.

(1) Everyone has the right to freedom of peaceful assembly and association.

(2) No one may be compelled to belong to an association.

Article 21.

(1) Everyone has the right to take part in the government of his country, directly or through freely chosen representatives.

(2) Everyone has the right of equal access to public service in his country.

(3) The will of the people shall be the basis of the authority of government; this will shall be expressed in periodic and genuine elections which shall be by universal and equal suffrage and shall be held by secret vote or by equivalent free voting procedures.

Article 22.

Everyone, as a member of society, has the right to social security and is entitled to realization, through national effort and international co-operation and in accordance with the organization and resources of each State, of the economic, social and cultural rights indispensable for his dignity and the free development of his personality.

Article 23.

(1) Everyone has the right to work, to free choice of employment, to just and favourable conditions of work and to protection against unemployment.

(2) Everyone, without any discrimination, has the right to equal pay for equal work.

(3) Everyone who works has the right to just and favourable remuneration ensuring for himself and his family an existence worthy of human dignity, and supplemented, if necessary, by other means of social protection.

(4) Everyone has the right to form and to join trade unions for the protection of his interests.

Article 24.

Everyone has the right to rest and leisure, including reasonable limitation of working hours and periodic holidays with pay.

Article 25.

(1) Everyone has the right to a standard of living adequate for the health and well-being of himself and of his family, including food, clothing, housing and medical care and necessary social services, and the right to security in the event of unemployment, sickness, disability, widowhood, old age or other lack of livelihood in circumstances beyond his control.

(2) Motherhood and childhood are entitled to special care and assistance. All children, whether born in or out of wedlock, shall enjoy the same social protection.

Article 26.

(1) Everyone has the right to education. Education shall be free, at least in the elementary and fundamental stages. Elementary education shall be compulsory. Technical and professional education shall be made generally available and higher education shall be equally accessible to all on the basis of merit.

(2) Education shall be directed to the full development of the human personality and to the strengthening of respect for human rights and fundamental freedoms. It shall promote understanding, tolerance and friendship among all nations, racial or religious groups, and shall further the activities of the United Nations for the maintenance of peace.

(3) Parents have a prior right to choose the kind of education that shall be given to their children.

Article 27.

(1) Everyone has the right freely to participate in the cultural life of the community, to enjoy the arts and to share in scientific advancement and its benefits.

(2) Everyone has the right to the protection of the moral and material interests resulting from any scientific, literary or artistic production of which he is the author.

Article 28.

Everyone is entitled to a social and international order in which the rights and freedoms set forth in this Declaration can be fully realized.

Article 29.

(1) Everyone has duties to the community in which alone the free and full development of his personality is possible.

(2) In the exercise of his rights and freedoms, everyone shall be subject only to such limitations as are determined by law solely for the purpose of securing due recognition and respect for the rights and freedoms of others and of meeting the just requirements of morality, public order and the general welfare in a democratic society.

(3) These rights and freedoms may in no case be exercised contrary to the purposes and principles of the United Nations.

Article 30.

Nothing in this Declaration may be interpreted as implying for any State, group or person any right to engage in any activity or to perform any act aimed at the destruction of any of the rights and freedoms set forth herein.

Appendix 4:
Cairo Declaration on Human Rights in Islam

5 August 1990.

The Nineteenth Islamic Conference of Foreign Ministers (Session of Peace, Interdependence and Development), held in Cairo, Arab Republic of Egypt, from 9-14 Muharram 1411H (31 July to 5 August 1990),

Keenly aware of the place of mankind in Islam as vicegerent of Allah on Earth;

Recognizing the importance of issuing a Document on Human Rights in Islam that will serve as a guide for Member states in all aspects of life;

Having examined the stages through which the preparation of this draft Document has so far, passed and the relevant report of the Secretary General;

Having examined the Report of the Meeting of the Committee of Legal Experts held in Tehran from 26 to 28 December, 1989;

Agrees to issue the Cairo Declaration on Human Rights in Islam that will serve as a general guidance for Member States in the Field of human rights.

Reaffirming the civilizing and historical role of the Islamic Ummah which Allah made as the best community and which gave humanity a universal and well-balanced civilization, in which harmony is established between hereunder and the hereafter, knowledge is combined with faith, and to fulfill the expectations from this community to guide all humanity which is confused because of different and conflicting beliefs and ideologies and to provide solutions for all chronic problems of this materialistic civilization.

In contribution to the efforts of mankind to assert human rights, to protect man from exploitation and persecution, and to affirm his freedom and right to a dignified life in accordance with the Islamic Shari'ah.

Convinced that mankind which has reached an advanced stage in materialistic science is still, and shall remain, in dire need of faith to support its civilization as well as a self motivating force to guard its rights;

Believing that fundamental rights and freedoms according to Islam are an integral part of the Islamic religion and that no one shall have the right as a matter of principle to abolish them either in whole or in part or to violate or ignore them in as much as they are binding divine commands, which are contained in the Revealed Books of Allah and which were sent through the last of His Prophets to complete the preceding divine messages and that safeguarding those fundamental rights and freedoms is an act of worship whereas the neglect or violation thereof is an abominable sin, and that the safeguarding of those fundamental rights and freedom is an individual responsibility of every person and a collective responsibility of the entire Ummah;

Do hereby and on the basis of the above-mentioned principles declare as follows:

Article 1.

(a) All human beings form one family whose members are united by their subordination to Allah and descent from Adam. All men are equal in terms of basic human dignity and basic obligations and responsibilities, without any discrimination on the basis of race, colour, language, belief, sex, religion, political affiliation, social status or other considerations. The true religion is the guarantee for enhancing such dignity along the path to human integrity.

(b) All human beings are Allah's subjects, and the most loved by Him are those who are most beneficial to His subjects, and no one has superiority over another except on the basis of piety and good deeds

Article 2.

(a) Life is a God-given gift and the right to life is guaranteed to every human being. It is the duty of individuals, societies and states to safeguard this right against any violation, and it is prohibited to take away life except for a shari'ah prescribed reason.

(b) It is forbidden to resort to any means which could result in the genocidal annihilation of mankind.

(c) The preservation of human life throughout the term of time willed by Allah is a duty prescribed by Shari'ah.

(d) Safety from bodily harm is a guaranteed right. It is the duty of the state to safeguard it, and it is prohibited to breach it without a Shari'ah-prescribed reason.

Article 3.

(a) In the event of the use of force and in case of armed conflict, it is not permissible to kill non-belligerents such as old men, women and children. The wounded and the sick shall have the right to medical treatment; and prisoners of war shall have the right to be fed, sheltered and clothed. It is prohibited to mutilate or dismember dead bodies. It is required to exchange prisoners of war and to arrange visits or reunions of families separated by circumstances of war.

(b) It is prohibited to cut down trees, to destroy crops or livestock, to destroy the enemy's civilian buildings and installations by shelling, blasting or any other means.

Article 4.

Every human being is entitled to human sanctity and the protection of one's good name and honour during one's life and after one's death. The state and the society shall protect one's body and burial place from desecration.

Article 5.

(a) The family is the foundation of society, and marriage is the basis of making a family. Men and women have the right to marriage, and no restrictions stemming from race, colour or nationality shall prevent them from exercising this right.

(b) The society and the State shall remove all obstacles to marriage and facilitate it, and shall protect the family and safeguard its welfare.

Article 6.

(a) Woman is equal to man in human dignity, and has her own rights to enjoy as well as duties to perform, and has her own civil entity and financial independence, and the right to retain her name and lineage.

(b) The husband is responsible for the maintenance and welfare of the family.

Article 7.

(a) As of the moment of birth, every child has rights due from the parents, the society and the state to be accorded proper nursing, education and material, hygienic and moral care. Both the fetus and the mother must be safeguarded and accorded special care.

(b) Parents and those in such like capacity have the right to choose the type of education they desire for their children, provided they take into consideration the interest and future of the children in accordance with ethical values and the principles of the Shari'ah.

(c) Both parents are entitled to certain rights from their children, and relatives are entitled to rights from their kin, in accordance with the tenets of the shari'ah.

Article 8.

Every human being has the right to enjoy a legitimate eligibility with all its prerogatives and obligations in case such eligibility is lost or impaired, the person shall have the right to be represented by his/her guardian.

Article 9.

(a) The seeking of knowledge is an obligation and provision of education is the duty of the society and the State. The State shall ensure the availability of ways and means to acquire education and shall guarantee its diversity in the interest of the society so as to enable man to be acquainted with the religion of Islam and uncover the secrets of the Universe for the benefit of mankind.

(b) Every human being has a right to receive both religious and worldly education from the various institutions of teaching, education and guidance, including the family, the school, the university, the media, etc., and in such an integrated and balanced manner that would develop human personality, strengthen man's faith in Allah and promote man's respect to and defence of both rights and obligations.

Article 10.

Islam is the religion of true unspoiled nature. It is prohibited to exercise any form of pressure on man or to exploit his poverty or ignorance in order to force him to change his religion to another religion or to atheism.

Article 11.

(a) Human beings are born free, and no one has the right to enslave, humiliate, oppress or exploit them, and there can be no subjugation but to Allah the Almighty.

(b) Colonialism of all types being one of the most evil forms of enslavement is totally prohibited. Peoples suffering from colonialism have the full right to freedom and self-determination.

It is the duty of all States peoples to support the struggle of colonized peoples for the liquidation of all forms of and occupation, and all States and peoples have the right to preserve their independent identity and control over their wealth and natural resources.

Article 12.

Every man shall have the right, within the framework of the Shari'ah, to free movement and to select his place of residence whether within or outside his country and if persecuted, is entitled to seek asylum in another country. The country of refuge shall be obliged to provide protection to the asylum-seeker until his safety has been attained, unless asylum is motivated by committing an act regarded by the Shari'ah as a crime.

Article 13.

Work is a right guaranteed by the State and the Society for each person with capability to work. Everyone shall be free to choose the work that suits him best and which serves his interests as well as those of the society. The employee shall have the right to enjoy safety and security as well as all other social guarantees. He may not be assigned work beyond his capacity nor shall he be subjected to compulsion or exploited or harmed in any way. He shall be entitled – without any discrimination between males and females – to fair wages for his work without delay, as well as to the holidays allowances and promotions which he deserves. On his part, he shall be required to be dedicated and meticulous in his work. Should workers and employers disagree on any matter, the State shall intervene to settle the dispute and have the grievances redressed, the rights confirmed and justice enforced without bias.

Article 13.

Everyone shall have the right to earn a legitimate living without monopolization, deceit or causing harm to oneself or to others.

Usury (riba) is explicitly prohibited.

Article 14.

(a) Everyone shall have the right to own property acquired in a legitimate way, and shall be entitled to the rights of ownership without prejudice to oneself, others or the society in general.

Expropriation is not permissible except for requirements of public interest and upon payment of prompt and fair compensation.

(b) Confiscation and seizure of property is prohibited except for a necessity dictated by law.

Article 15.

Everyone shall have the right to enjoy the fruits of his scientific, literary, artistic or technical labour of which he is the author; and he shall have the right to the protection of his moral and material interests stemming therefrom, provided it is not contrary to the principles of the Shari'ah.

Article 16.

(a) Everyone shall have the right to live in a clean environment, away from vice and moral corruption, that would favour a healthy ethical development of his person and it is incumbent upon the State and society in general to afford that right.

(b) Everyone shall have the right to medical and social care, and to all public amenities provided by society and the State within the limits of their available resources.

(c) The States shall ensure the right of the individual to a decent living that may enable him to meet his requirements and those of his dependents, including food, clothing, housing, education, medical care and all other basic needs.

Article 17.

(a) Everyone shall have the right to live in security for himself, his religion, his dependents, his honour and his property.

(b) Everyone shall have the right to privacy in the conduct of his private affairs, in his home, among his family, with regard to his property and his relationships. It is not permitted to spy on him, to place him under surveillance or to besmirch his good name. The State shall protect him from arbitrary interference.

(c) A private residence is inviolable in all cases. It will not be entered without permission from its inhabitants or in any unlawful manner, nor shall it be demolished or confiscated and its dwellers evicted.

Article 18.

(a) All individuals are equal before the law, without distinction between the ruler and the ruled.

(b) The right to resort to justice is guaranteed to everyone.

(c) Liability is in essence personal.

(d) There shall be no crime or punishment except as provided for in the Shari'ah.

(e) A defendant is innocent until his guilt is proven in a fast trial in which he shall be given all the guarantees of defence.

Article 19.

It is not permitted without legitimate reason to arrest an individual, or restrict his freedom, to exile or to punish him. It is not permitted to subject him to physical or psychological torture or to any form of maltreatment, cruelty or indignity. Nor is it permitted to subject an individual to medical or scientific experiments without his consent or at the risk of his health or of his life. Nor is it permitted to promulgate emergency laws that would provide executive authority for such actions.

Article 20.

Taking hostages under any form or for any purpose is expressly forbidden.

Article 21.

(a) Everyone shall have the right to express his opinion freely in such manner as would not be contrary to the principles of the Shari'ah.

(b) Everyone shall have the right to advocate what is right, and propagate what is good, and warn against what is wrong and evil according to the norms of Islamic Shari'ah.

(c) Information is a vital necessity to society. It may not be exploited or misused in such a way as may violate sanctities and the dignity of Prophets, undermine moral and ethical Values or disintegrate, corrupt or harm society or weaken its faith.

(d) It is not permitted to excite nationalistic or doctrinal hatred or to do anything that may be an incitement to any form or racial discrimination.

Article 23.

(a) Authority is a trust; and abuse or malicious exploitation thereof is explicitly prohibited, in order to guarantee fundamental human rights.

(b) Everyone shall have the right to participate, directly or indirectly in the administration of his country's public affairs. He shall also have the right to assume public office in accordance with the provisions of Shari'ah.

Article 24.

All the rights and freedoms stipulated in this Declaration are subject to the Islamic Shari'ah.

Article 25.

The Islamic Shari'ah is the only source of reference for the explanation or clarification of any of the articles of this Declaration.

Copyright © University Committee on Human Rights at Harvard, 2002

Glossary

'adhab^{un} 'azim^{un} – a dreadful penalty from God that is the lot of apostates according to Qur'an 16:106.

Ahmadis – members of a Muslim sect, the Ahmadiyya, originating in 19th-century India, regarded as extremely heretical by other Muslims

Allah – God; used by all Muslims and by Arabic-speaking Christians, but with different understandings of the nature and character of God

Baha'i – a religious movement that arose as an offshoot of Shi'a Islam in late 19th-century Iran but now considers itself a separate world religion; considered heretical by most Muslims and severely persecuted in Iran

bid'a – a forbidden innovation in Islam

fai' – property that was taken from non-Muslims without fighting and put in the state treasury

fatwa – an authoritative statement on a point of Islamic law

fiqh – Islamic jurisprudence, the science of applying Islamic law

fuqaha (sing. *faqih*) – experts in Islamic jurisprudence who can derive applications of shari'a for contemporary cases

hadd (pl. *hudud*) – specific punishments laid down in the Qur'an for certain specific crimes "against religion", and therefore mandatory under Islamic law

hadith – traditions recording what Muhammad and his followers said and did; some of the various collections are considered more authentic and reliable than others

hadith ahad – a tradition of Muhammad that is narrated by fewer people than that of a totally reliable one (*hadith mutawatir*)

145

hadith mutawatir – a totally reliable tradition narrated by such a
large number of people that they cannot all be supposed to have
agreed upon a lie

Hanafi – a Sunni school of shari'a, founded by Imam abu Hanifa
(died 767)

Hanbali – a Sunni school of shari'a, founded by Imam abu Ahmad
ibn Hanbal (died 855)

haram – forbidden or unlawful according to shari'a; the opposite of
halal (permitted)

hiraba – armed robbery, a crime falling under the *hudud* laws of
shari'a and requiring the death penalty by crucifixion or amputation of limbs and imprisonment

hisba – legal shari'a principle stating that each Muslim has the responsibility to enforce Islamic behaviour (commanding good and pro-
hibiting evil) in his community; primarily the duty of the state,
leading in modern Muslim states to the religious police enforcing
piety and morality

'ibadat – shari'a rules pertaining to humans' duties to God, thus
mainly to ritual and worship, including ritual purity, prayer, alms,
fasting, pilgrimage and jihad

hudud – see *hadd*

ijma' – the consensus of Muslim scholars on any point of Islamic law

ijtihad – an "effort" or legal procedure to understand and apply the
Qur'an and *hadith* to circumstances not addressed directly or by
direct analogy; used to create shari'a

irtidad – apostasy from Islam

Islamism – a view of Islam as a comprehensive political ideology that
aims at establishing Islamic states under shari'a; characterised by
zeal, activism and following shari'a in minute detail

Ja'fari – the Shi'a school of Islamic law

jihad – literally "striving"; the term has various interpretations,
including (1) spiritual struggle for moral purity, (2) trying to cor-
rect wrong and support right by voice and actions, (3) military war
against non-Muslims with the aim of spreading Islam

kafir – infidel, i.e. non-Muslim; a term of gross insult

kufr – unbelief (includes apostasy, blasphemy and heresy)

madhahib (sing. *madhab*) – recognised orthodox Islamic schools of
law codified in the 10th century; the four Sunni *madhahib*, named

after their founders, are the Hanafi, Maliki, Shafi'i and Hanbali;
the Shi'a *madhab* is also called the Ja'fari.

Maliki – a Sunni school of shari'a, founded by Imam Malik ibn Anas
(died 795)

mu'amallat – shari'a rules pertaining to social relations and including
criminal law, family law, economic law, etc

munafiqun – hypocrites, originally in Muhammad's Medina a
group of converts to Islam who later relapsed or connived with
Muhammad's enemies; accused of pretending to be Muslims out-
wardly while in fact being apostates

murtadd – an apostate from Islam

qisas – retaliation, a principle of shari'a criminal law by which the
offender is punished by the infliction of the exact damage caused
to the victim; in the case of murder, the next of kin of the victim have the right to demand the death penalty; they can however
also demand the payment of blood money in lieu of the offender's
execution

qiyas – reasoning by analogy, used in *ijtihad*

Qur'an – the holy book of Islam, comprising a series of "revelations"
that Muhammad believed God gave him between 610 and 632

ridda – to apostatise from Islam

Shafi'i – a Sunni school of shari'a, founded by Imam Muhammad bin
Idris ash Shafi'i (died 820)

shari'a – literally "the way"; Islamic law

Shi'a – the second largest branch of Islam, which broke away from
the main body in 657

sira – biography of Muhammad, especially any of the authoritative
early accounts

sunna – literally "the trodden path"; the actions, words and way of life
of Muhammad as recorded in the *hadith*, as the supreme example
for Muslims to follow; some Muslims also include the actions and
words of his early followers who knew him personally

Sunni – the largest branch of Islam, comprising more than 80% of
Muslims today

sura – a chapter of the Qur'an

ta'zir – a part of shari'a in which the judge has discretionary powers in deciding on the punishment of the offender (as opposed to
hudud where the punishment is prescribed)

tafsir – classical Islamic genre of books interpreting the meaning of the Qur'anic text

takfir – the legal process of declaring that a Muslim individual, community or institution is an apostate or infidel, worthy of death

'ulama (sing. *alim*) – scholars and religious authorities, skilled in the study of Islam

umma – the community or nation of Islam, composed of all Muslims worldwide

Wahhabi – member of a puritanical reform movement of Sunni Islam founded in the 18th century AD and dominant in Saudi Arabia

Zandaqah – an early category of heresy in Islam, mainly concerning Muslims who secretly accepted Manichean beliefs

Zindiq – a person belonging to the category of heresy known as *Zandaqah*

Endnotes

1   General Assembly of U.N., *Universal Declaration of Human Rights*, Article 18.

2   A Kuwaiti jurist (1996) quoted in Anh Nga Longva, "The Apostasy Law in the Age of Universal Human Rights and Citizenship: Some Legal and Political Implications", paper delivered at the Fourth Nordic Conference on Middle Eastern Studies: The Middle East in a Globalizing World, Oslo, 13-16 August 1998, http://www.hf.uib.no/smi/pao/longva.html.

3   Mohamed S. El-Awa, *Punishment in Islamic Law: A Contemporary Study.* Plainfield: American Trust Publications, 2000, pp49-50, 53.

4   Muhammad Iqbal Siddiqi, *The Penal Law of Islam*. Lahore: Kazi Publications, 1979, p97.

5   Abul A'la Mawdudi, *The Punishment of the Apostate According to Islamic Law*. Lahore: Islamic Publications, 1963. English translation by Syed Silas Husain & Ernest Hahn, 1994, p17.

6   Rudolph Peters & Gert J.J. De Vries, "Apostasy in Islam", *Die Welt des Islams,* Vol. XVII: No. 1-4, 1976-7, pp14-18.

7   Y. 'Ali, *The Holy Qur'an*. Leicester: The Islamic Foundation, 1975, p1729.

8   S. Zwemer, *The Law of Apostasy in Islam*. London: Marshall Brothers Ltd, 1924, p34.

9   Zwemer, *The Law of Apostasy in Islam*, pp34-35.

10   H. Gibb and J. Kramers, *Shorter Encyclopaedia of Islam*. Leiden: E.J. Brill, 1974, p413.

11   Siddiqi, *The Penal Law of Islam*, p97.

12   Mawdudi, *The Punishment of the Apostate According to Islamic Law*, pp18-19.

13   Zwemer, *The Law of Apostasy in Islam*, pp33-34.

14   *The Meaning of the Glorious Qur'an*, An explanatory translation by Mohammad Marmaduke Pickthall. Birmingham: UK Islamic Mission Dawah Centre, 2000, p100, fn1.

15   'Ali, *The Holy Qur'an*, p207, fn606.

16   S.A. Rahman, *Punishment of Apostasy in Islam*. Lahore: Institute of Islamic Culture, 1978, pp5-17. He claims that Ibn al-'Arabi, Zamakhshari and al-

Baydawi held this view. See also the discussion in El-Awa, *Punishment in Islamic Law*, pp50-51.

17 *Tafsir al-Qurtubi: Classical Commentary on the Holy Qur'an*, translated by Aisha Bewley, Vol. 1. London: Dar al-Taqwa, 2003, pp659-661.

18 *Tafsir al-Qurtubi: Classical Commentary on the Holy Qur'an*, p661.

19 See Rahman, *Punishment of Apostasy in Islam*, pp16-25. Rahman on p16 declares this verse to be "one of the most important verses of the Qur'an, containing a charter of freedom of conscience unparalleled in the religious annals of mankind..." He goes on to criticise the attempts by Muslim scholars over the ages to narrow its broad humanistic meaning and impose limits on its scope in their attempts to reconcile it with their interpretations of Muhammad's *Sunna*.

20 *Tafsir Ibn Kathir* (Abridged), Vol. 2. Riyadh: Darussalam Publishers, 2000, pp30-31; Abdullah Saeed and Hassan Saeed, *Freedom of Religion in Islam*. Aldershot, Hants: Ashgate, 2004, pp73-78; Yohanan Friedmann, *Tolerance and Coercion in Islam*. Cambridge: Cambridge University Press, 2003, pp100-106.

21 Ali Khan, "The Reopening of the Islamic Code: The Second Era of Ijtihad", *University of St. Thomas Law Journal*, 2003, http://washburnlaw.edu/faculty/khan-a-fulltext/2003-1univstthomlj341.pdf (viewed 15 July 2009).

22 El-Awa, *Punishment in Islamic Law*, p51.

23 El-Awa, *Punishment in Islamic Law*, p52.

24 A category of defining *hadith* according to the reliability of their transmitters. A weak *hadith* is not to be rejected outright, but one must find whether the transmitter's traditions are supported elsewhere.

25 El-Awa, *Punishment in Islamic Law*, p52.

26 El-Awa, *Punishment in Islamic Law*, pp51-52.

27 Quoted in M. Mukarram Ahmed, ed., *Encyclopaedia of Islam*, Vol. 10. New Delhi: Anmol Publications, 2005, p364.

28 Quoted in Siddiqi, *The Penal Law of Islam*, pp103-104.

29 Quoted in Zwemer, *The Law of Apostasy in Islam*, p50.

30 Saeed and Saeed, *Freedom of Religion*, pp55-56.

31 *The Hedaya: Commentary on the Islamic Laws*, Vol. II, translated by Charles Hamilton. New Delhi: Nusratali Nasri for Kitab Bhavan, reprinted 1985, Appendix A.

32 *The Hedaya*, Vol. II, p225.

33 *The Hedaya*, Vol. II, p225.

34 *The Hedaya*, Vol. II, pp225-226.

35 *The Hedaya*, Vol. II, p245.

36 *The Hedaya*, Vol. II, p246; Siddiqi, *The Penal Law of Islam*, p110.

37 *The Hedaya*, Vol. II, pp239, 244-5

38 *The Hedaya*, Vol. II, p244

39 *The Hedaya*, Vol. II, p231.

40 *The Hedaya*, Vol. II, p227.

41 *The Hedaya*, Vol. II, p.227.

42 *The Hedaya*, Vol. II, p246; Siddiqi, *The Penal Law of Islam*, p110.

43 *The Hedaya*, Vol. II, p236.

44 *The Hedaya*, Vol. II, p232.

45 *The Hedaya*, Vol II, p228.

46 *The Hedaya*, Vol. II, p22.

47 *The Hedaya*, Vol. II, p232.

48 *The Hedaya*, Vol. II, pp235-236.

49 *The Hedaya*, Vol. II, p238.

50 *The Hedaya*, Vol. II, p232.

51 'Abdullah ibn Abi Zayd al-Qayrawani, *Al-Risala*, translated by Alhaj Bello Mohammad Daura, 37.19, http://www.iiu.edu.my/deed/lawbase/risalah_maliki/book37.html (viewed 10 November 2008); F.H. Ruxton, "Convert's Status in Maliki Law", *The Moslem World*, Vol. III, p38, quoted in Zwemer, *The Law of Apostasy in Islam*, p42.

52 Heretics are Muslims with beliefs that are held by the orthodox majority to be deviant. Hypocrites pretend to be good Muslims but in their hearts do not really believe. Apostates have left Islam for another religion.

53 Ruxton, "Convert's Status", quoted in Zwemer, *The Law of Apostasy in Islam*, p43.

54 Quoted in Zwemer, *The Law of Apostasy in Islam*, pp47-50.

55 Nawawi, "*Minhaj-at-Talibin*", quoted in Zwemer, *The Law of Apostasy in Islam*, p49.

56 Ahmad ibn Naqib al-Misri, *The Reliance of the Traveller: A Classic Manual Of Islamic Sacred Law*, translated by Nuh Ha Mim Keller, new edition. Beltsville, Maryland: amana publications, 1997, pp595-596.

57 Anwar Ahmad Qadri, *A Sunnin Shafi'i Law Code*. Lahore: SH: Muhammad Ashraf, 1984, p123.

58 Quoted in Zwemer, *The Law of Apostasy in Islam*, pp47-50

59 John Witte and J.D. Van der Vyver, eds., *Religious Human Rights in Global Perspective: Legal Perspective*. The Hague: Martinus Nijhoff Publishers, 1996, p406, Note 66.

60 Joseph Schacht, *An Introduction to Islamic Law*. London: Oxford University Press, 1964, p16.

61 A. Querry, *Recueil de Lois concernant Les Musulmans Schyites*, Vol. II, quoted in Zwemer, *The Law of Apostasy in Islam*, p51.

62 Querry, *Recueil de Lois concernant Les Musulmans Schyites*, quoted in Zwemer, *The*

Law of Apostasy in Islam, p51.

63 Querry, *Recueil de Lois concernant Les Musulmans Schyites*, quoted in Zwemer, *The Law of Apostasy in Islam*, p51.

64 Ibn Warraq, "Apostasy and Human Rights", International Humanist and Ethical Union, 21 June 2005, http://www.iheu.org/node/1541 (viewed 2 June 2009).

65 Qadi 'Iyad Ibn Musa al-Yahsubi, *Muhammad: Messenger of Allah (Ash-Shifa of Qadi 'Iyad)*, translated by Aisha Abdurrahman Bewley. Inverness: Madinah Press, 1991, pp375-376.

66 Al-Yahsubi, *Muhammad*, p410.

67 Al-Yahsubi, *Muhammad*, p412.

68 Abdul Hameed Abu Sulayman , "Al-dhimmah and Related Concepts in Historical Perspective", *Journal Institute of Muslim Minority Affairs*, Vol. 9: No. 1, January 1988, pp18-19.

69 Zwemer, *The Law of Apostasy in Islam*, p35.

70 S. Mahmassani, *Arkan huquq al-insan*. Beirut: Dar al-'ilm li'l-malayin, 1979, pp123-124. Reference in Ann Elizabeth Mayer, *Islam and Human Rights: Tradition and Politics*. Boulder, Colorado: Westview Press and London: Pinter Publishers, 1991, p170.

71 Zaki Badawi, "Freedom of Religion in Islam", unpublished paper presented 10 January 2003. (See Appendix 2.)

72 Zaki Badawi, "Freedom of Religion in Islam".

73 El-Awa, *Punishment in Islamic Law*, pp54-64.

74 *Sunday*, BBC Radio 4, 12 May 1991.

75 Mawdudi, *The Punishment of the Apostate According to Islamic Law*, pp46-49.

76 Abdurahman Abdulkadir Kurdi, *The Islamic State: A Study based on the Islamic Holy Constitution*. London: Mansell Publishing Limited, 1984, pp52-53.

77 Siddiqi, *The Penal Law of Islam*, pp108-109.

78 Sheikh Muhammad Abu Zahra, "Punishment in Islam", in D.F. Green, ed., *Arab Theologians on Jews and Israel: Extracts from the Proceedings of the Fourth Conference of the Academy of Islamic Research*, 3rd edition. Geneva: Editions de l'Avenir, 1976, pp71-72.

79 "Source of the Punishment for Apostasy", http://islamonline.net/fatwaapplication/english/display.asp?hFatwaID=102152 (viewed 10 August 2005).

80 Yusuf al-Qaradawi, *Islamic Awakening Between Rejection and Extremism*, new edition. Herndon, VA: International Institute of Islamic Thought, 2006, p45.

81 Saeed and Saeed, *Freedom of Religion*, pp44, 48-49.

82 Patrick Sookhdeo, *A People Betrayed: The Impact of Islamization on the Christian Community in Pakistan*. Fearn, Ross-shire: Christian Focus Publications and Pewsey, Wiltshire: Isaac Publishing, 2002, p243.

83 Sookhdeo, *A People Betrayed*, pp297-302.

84 Rudolph Peters, *Crime and Punishment in Islamic Law*. Cambridge: Cambridge University Press, 2005, p180; Muhammad Asrar Madani, *Verdict of Islamic Law on Blasphemy & Apostasy*. Lahore: Idara-e-Islamiat, 1994, pp19-20.

85 From al-Saif al-Sarim, Vol. 2, p. 194, quoted in Madani, *Verdict of Islamic Law*, p71.

86 www.light-of-life.com/eng/ilaw/15721et3.htm (viewed 21 June 2002).

87 Quoted in Madani, *Verdict of Islamic Law*, p117.

88 Quoted in Madani, *Verdict of Islamic Law*, p117.

89 Quoted in Madani, *Verdict of Islamic Law*, p118.

90 Al-Yahsubi, *Muhammad*, pp373-374.

91 Al-Yahsubi, *Muhammad*, p374.

92 Al-Yahsubi, *Muhammad*, pp374-375.

93 Al-Yahsubi, *Muhammad*, pp.373-376, 386.

94 John L. Esposito, ed., *The Oxford Encyclopedia of the Modern Islamic World*. New York: The Oxford University Press, 1995, pp439-443.

95 Badawi, "Freedom of Religion in Islam".

96 El-Awa, *Punishment in Islamic Law*, p53.

97 El-Awa, *Punishment in Islamic Law*, pp54-64.

98 Ali A. Allawi, *The Crisis of Islamic Civilization*. New Haven and London: Yale University Press, 2009.

99 Allawi, *The Crisis of Islamic Civilization*, pp10-15.

100 Ann Elizabeth Mayer, *Islam and Human Rights: Tradition and Politics*. Boulder, Colorado: Westview Press and London: Pinter Publishers, 1991, pp172-173.

101 Allawi, *The Crisis of Islamic Civilization*, pp191-192.

102 Allawi, *The Crisis of Islamic Civilization*, pp191-192.

103 Allawi, *The Crisis of Islamic Civilization*, pp192-193.

104 "Egypt Mufti denies saying Muslims can choose own religion", AFP, 24 July 2007, http://www.haaba.com/news-story/egypt-mufti-denies-saying-muslims-can-choose-own-religion (viewed 3 November 2008); Ali Gomaa, "Freedom of Religion in Islam", http://newsweek.washingtonpost.com/onfaith/muslims_speak_out/2007/07/sheikh_ali_gomah.html (viewed 29 August 2007); "Egypt mufti says Muslims are free to change faith", *The Straits Times*, 25 July 2007.

105 Abdullah Saeed, *Muslim Australians: Their Beliefs, Practices and Institutions*. Canberra: Commonwealth of Australia, Department Of Immigration And Multicultural And Indigenous Affairs And Australian Multicultural Foundation In Association With The University Of Melbourne, 2004.

106 Saeed, *Muslim Australians*, p72. For an evaluation of Saeed's doubletalk see: Peter Day,

"Australian Apologetics for Islam", *Quadrant Online*, 2009/5, http://www.quadrant. org.au/magazine/issue/2009/5/australian-apologetics-for-islam (viewed 20 May 2009).

107 Saeed and Saeed, *Freedom of Religion*.

108 Saeed and Saeed, *Freedom of Religion*, p88.

109 Saeed and Saeed, *Freedom of Religion*, p2.

110 Patrick Goodenough, "Islamic Scholars Wrestle With Death-For-Apostasy Issue", *CNSNews*, 30 April 2009, http://www.cnsnews.com/Public/content/article. aspx?RsrcID=47401 (viewed 22 May 2009); Badea Abu Al-Naja, "Scholars hotly debate treatment of apostates", *Arab News*, 30 April 2009; Badea Abu Al-Naja, "Freedom of expression should not be misused", *Arab News*, 2 May 2009.

111 The Egyptian Constitution states in article 2: "Islam is the Religion of the State. Arabic is its official language, and the principal source of legislation is Islamic Jurisprudence (Sharia)." Egyptian Parliament website, http://www.parliament.gov. eg/EPA/en/itemX.jsp?itemFlag=%22Strange%22&categoryID=1&sectionID=11&t ypeID=1&categoryIDX=1&itemID=8&levelid=54&parentlevel=6&levelno=2. The Mauritanian Constitution of 1991 states in its Preamble that the precepts of Islam are the only source of law. "Mauritania – Constitution", ICL Document, 12 July 1991, http://www.oefre.unibe.ch/law/icl/mr00000_.html (viewed 11 November 2008).

112 For instance, in Egypt certain high public positions are closed to Christians by an unwritten rule, while churches need special permits for the minutest renovations. In Pakistan religious minorities suffer from "arbitrary denial of social and economic rights as well as the rights to preach, practice and propagate minority beliefs" as well as being subject to many kinds of harassment and humiliation. "Pakistan: Insufficient Protection of Religious Minorities", *Amnesty International*, May 2001, ASA 33/008/2001, pp25-28.

113 Azzam Tamimi, "Human Rights – Islamic and Secular Perspectives", in Abdul Wahid Hamid and Jamil Sherif (eds.), *The Quest for Sanity*. London: The Muslim Council of Britain, 2002, pp229-235.

114 Daveed Gartenstein-Ross, "When Muslims Convert", *Commentary*, Vol. 119, No. 2, February 2005.

115 "Summary Record of the 1251st Meeting: Iran (Islamic Republic of), 29/07/93", *United Nations, International Covenant on Civil and Political Rights (CCPR)*.

116 Christine Schirrmacher, "Human Rights in Muslim Understanding", http://www. hfe.org/news/profiles/islam_rights.htm.

117 An example of incitement to mob violence based on a false accusation of blasphemy (Christians were falsely accused of tearing and burning pages of the Qur'an as well as of writing blasphemous statements on them), is documented in Sookhdeo, *A People Betrayed*, pp268-274. Large mobs of infuriated Muslims led by clerics and armed with

sticks, axes, knives, firearms, explosives and petrol bombs attacked the Christians in the village of Shanti Nagar in the Punjab, Pakistan, on 5 and 6 February 1997, looting houses and setting them on fire, and destroying telephone and electricity connections as well as water supplies. Also a number of Christian women were abducted.

118 See the following case studies, especially those under the heading "Muslim Intellectuals Seen as Deviating from Orthodox Interpretations of Islam".

119 "Pakistan: Insufficient Protection of Religious Minorities", pp2-4, 28-29.

120 A useful work that illuminates this is Hazrat Mirza Tahir Ahmad, *Murder in the Name of Allah*. Cambridge: Lutterworth Press, 1989. Ahmad is the supreme spiritual head of the Ahmadiyya sect, which has been severely suppressed in Pakistan. Similarly, the liberal and reformist Sudanese group, the Republican Brothers, officially became apostates from Islam under the Nimeiri regime, although they themselves believed they were Muslims following Islamic teaching.

121 Al-Yahsubi, *Muhammad*, p410.

122 David G. Littman, "'Submission' at the United Nations?", Pim Fortuyn Memorial Conference on Islam, The Hague, 17-19 February 2005.

123 David G. Littman, "Islamism Grows Stronger at the United Nations", *Middle East Quarterly*, September 1999, pp59-64.

124 The UNHRC is composed of 47 states, of which 17 are Muslim. Founded in 2006 to replace the UNCHR, it has no power beyond drawing international attention to rights issues and abuses in certain countries.

125 The UN General Assembly resolutions are not legally binding on its 192 member states, but pave the way for the formation of multilateral treaties and customary international law.

126 Liaquat Ali Khan, "Combating Defamation of Religions", MWC News, 18 April 2008.

127 "Shattering The Red Lines: The Durban II Draft Declaration", UN Watch, October 2008, www.unwatch.org/durban2 (viewed 23 April 2009).

128 "Combating the Defamation of Religions", Resolution adopted by the General Assembly of the United Nations, 62/154, 6 March 2008.

129 "Proposal at UN to criminalize 'defamation of religion'", UN Watch Briefing, issue 190, 11 March 2009.

130 Saeed and Saeed, *Freedom of Religion*, pp109, 116.

131 "Indonesia: Radicalisation of the 'Palembang Group'", *International Crisis Group*, Asia Briefing No. 92, Jakarta / Brussels, 20 May 2009.

132 "Defying World Trends: Saudi Arabia's Extensive Use of Capital Punishment", *Amnesty International* report based on a paper compiled by Amnesty International for the 1st World Congress Against the Death Penalty, 21-23 June 2001, Strasbourg.

133 Sookhdeo, *A People Betrayed*, pp257-274.

134 "Pakistan: Insufficient Protection of Religious Minorities", pp57-60.

135 Members of a Muslim group founded in the 19th century, regarded as heretical by most "orthodox" Muslims and proclaimed a non-Muslim minority by the Pakistani authorities in 1974. Legislation in 1984 made it a criminal offence for Ahmadis to call themselves Muslim. See "Pakistan: Insufficient Protection of Religious Minorities", pp2-3.

136 Akbar S. Ahmed, "Pakistan's Blasphemy Law: Words Fail Me", *Washington Post*, 19 May 2002, pB1.

137 Ahmed, "Pakistan's Blasphemy Law", pB1.

138 "Persecuted Minorities and Writers in Pakistan", *Human Rights Watch*, Vol. 5, Number 13, 19 September 1993.

139 "Pakistani court frees 'blasphemer' ", *BBC News*, Thursday 15 August 2002, http://news.bbc.co.uk/1/low/world/south_asia/2196275.stm.

140 "Persecution Under the Blasphemy Laws in Pakistan", *Jubilee Campaign* Information Sheet, http://www.jubileecampaign.co.uk/world/pak25.htm.

141 Sookhdeo, *A People Betrayed*, pp239-243, 249-257; "Pakistan: Insufficient Protection of Religious Minorities".

142 Idrees Bakhtiar, "Karachi police break up blasphemy rally", *BBC News*, Wednesday 10 January 2001, http://news.bbc.co.uk/1/hi/world/south_asia/1110187.stm; "Critics condemn Pakistani government retraction", *BBC News*, Wednesday 17 May 2000, http://news.bbc.co.uk/1/hi/world/south_asia/752532.stm.

143 "Religious Freedom in the Majority Islamic Countries, 1998 Report: Egypt", *Aid to the Church in Need*, http://www.alleanzacattolica.org/acs/acs_english/report_98/egypt.htm; Fauzi M. Najjar, "Book Banning in Contemporary Egypt", *The Muslim World*, Vol. 91, Nos. 3&4, Fall 2001.

144 See Hebatallah Ghali, "Rights of Muslim Converts to Christianity in Egypt", MA thesis submitted to The American University in Cairo, Department of Law, December 2006, pp4, 8-9, Appendix pp1-2.

145 Mayer, *Islam and Human Rights*, p169.

146 Najjar, "Book Banning in Contemporary Egypt".

147 See the series of articles on the punishment for apostasy by Sayyed Al-Qimni in *Rose El-Youssef*, weeks 40-44, 2002. See also Najjar, "Book Banning in Contemporary Egypt".

148 Harvey Glickman, "Islamism in Sudan's Civil War", *Orbis*, Vol. 44, No. 2, Spring 2000, pp267-282.

149 The1998 Constitution of Sudan, Article IV, Chapter I "Sources of legislation", article 65, states: "Islamic law and the consensus of the nation, by referendum,

Constitution and custom shall be the sources of legislation ; and no legislation in contravention with these fundamentals shall be made."

150 Abdullahi Ahmed An-Na'im, "Application of Shari'ah (Islamic Law) and Human Rights Violations in the Sudan", in *Religion and Human Rights: Proceedings of the Conference Convened by the Sudan Human Rights Organization*, 1992, p101; "Sudan", International Religious Freedom Report, US Department of State, 2001; "Persecuted Church News - Sudan: 'Religious Freedom'? Not Really!", *World Evangelical Alliance, Religious Liberty Prayer List*, No. 158, March 2002, http://www.worldevangelical.org/persec_sudan_06mar02.html.

151 "Summary Record of the 1629th Meeting: Sudan, 31/10/97", *United Nations, International Covenant on Civil and Political Rights (CCPR).*

152 "Sudan", International Religious Freedom Report, US Department of State, 2008, http://www.state.gov/g/drl/rls/irf/2008/108393.htm (viewed 29 Oct 2008).

153 "Summary Record of the 1251st Meeting: Iran (Islamic Republic of), 29/07/93", *United Nations, International Covenant on Civil and Political Rights (CCPR).*

154 "Iran: A legal System that Fails to Protect Freedom of Expression and Association", *Amnesty International*, AI-index: MDE 13/045/2001, http://web.amnesty.org/ai.nsf/Index/MDE130452001?OpenDocument&of=COUNTRIES/IRAN.

155 Saeed and Saeed, *Freedom of Religion*, pp126-127.

156 A.R. Embong, "The Culture and Practice of Pluralism in Post-Colonial Malaysia", in Robert W. Hefner (ed.), *The Politics of Multiculturalism: Pluralism and Citizenship in Malaysia, Singapore, and Indonesia*. Grand Rapids, MI: William B. Eerdmans, 2002, pp74-75.

157 Robert W. Hefner, "Introduction", in Hefner (ed.), *Multiculturalism*, pp22-24.

158 Robert Day McAmis, *Malay Muslims: The History and Challenge of Resurgent Islam in Southeast Asia*. Honolulu: University of Hawai'i Press, 2001, pp85-90. "NECF Malaysia's Response To The Lina Joy Judgement", National Evangelical Christian Fellowship press statement, 1 June 2007, http://www.necf.org.my/newsmaster.cfm?&menuid=43&action=view&retrieveid=874 (viewed 31 October 2008).

159 "NECF Malaysia's Response To The Lina Joy Judgement", *National Evangelical Christian Fellowship* press statement, 1 June 2007, http://www.necf.org.my/newsmaster.cfm?&menuid=43&action=view&retrieveid=874 (viewed 31 October 2008).

160 Zainah Anwar, "What Islam, Whose Islam? Sisters in Islam and the Struggle for Women's Rights", in Hefner (ed.), *Multiculturalism*, pp235-236.

161 "Islam, Apostasy and PAS", *Sisters in Islam*, No. 6, July 1999, http://www.sistersin-islam.org.my/lettersto editors22071999.htm.

162 "International Religious Freedom Report 2008, Maldives", Bureau of Democracy,

Human Rights, and Labor, US Department of State, http://www.state.gov/g/drl/rls/irf/2008/108503.htm (viewed 31 October 2008).

163 Odd Larsen, "MALDIVES: Religious freedom survey, October 2008", *Forum 18 News Service*, 15 October 2008, http://www.forum18.org/Archive.php?article_id=1203 (viewed 31 October 2008).

164 Larsen, "MALDIVES".

165 Larsen, "MALDIVES".

166 Larsen, "MALDIVES".

167 Olivia Lang, "'Anni' heralds new era in Maldives", *BBC News*, 29 October 2008.

168 "Sudan: 'Religious Freedom'? Not Really!".

169 Human Rights Watch, "Crises in Sudan and Northern Uganda", Testimony of Jemera Rone, Human Rights Watch Before the House Subcommittee on International Operations and Human Rights and the Subcommittee on Africa, 29 July 1998, http://www.hrw.org/campaigns/sudan98/testim/house-01.htm; "Moslem Convert to Christianity faces death for 'apostasy' in Sudan", *Servant's Heart*, http://.blue-nile.org/news/980716_convert_ faces_death.htm.

170 "Iran, Religious and Ethnic Minorities: Discrimination in Law and in Practice", *Human Rights Watch*, http://www.hrw.org/reports/1997/iran/Iran-05.html.

171 "Iran, Religious and Ethnic Minorities".

172 Michael Nazir-Ali, "The Killing of Brother George", *The Guardian*, 29 July 2000; "The Geneva Report 2001: A Perspective on Religious Freedom: Challenges Facing the Christian Community", *World Evangelical Alliance, Religious Liberty Commission*, http://www.worldeavangelical.org/textonly/3rlc_genevareport01.htm.

173 Sookhdeo, *A People Betrayed*, pp264-267.

174 "Pakistan: Insufficient Protection of Religious Minorities"; "Another Christian Receives the Death Sentence for Blasphemy", *Barnabas Fund*, http;//www.pastor-net.nt.au/jmm/aame/aame0413.htm.

175 Amin Tarzi, "Afghanistan: Apostasy Case Reveals Constitutional Contradictions", *Radio Free Europe*, 22 March 2006, http://www.rferl.org/content/article/1066970.html (viewed 3 November 2008).

176 Afghan convert 'arrives in Italy', *BBC News*, 29 March 2006.

177 "Poster calling for death of lawyer involved in the Lina Joy case", *Asia News*, 22 September 2006; Sebastian Tong, "Malaysia's converts test freedom of faith", *Reuters*, 25 June 2006.

178 "Malaysia rejects Christian appeal", *BBC News*, 30 May 2007.

179 Gartenstein-Ross, "When Muslims Convert", pp66-68.

180 Ruth Gledhill, "British imam's daughter under police protection after converting to Christianity", *The Times*, 5 December 2007.

Endnotes

181 Ruth Gledhill, "British Muslim 'bullied' for converting to Christianity", *The Times*, 28 April 2008.

182 Anthony Browne, "Muslim apostates cast out and at risk from faith and family", *The Times*, 5 February 2005; Ruth Gledhill, "British Muslim 'bullied'".

183 Gledhill, "British imam's daughter"; Dominic Lawson, "My imam father came after me with an axe", *The Sunday Times*, 15 March 2009.

184 Gartenstein-Ross, "When Muslims Convert", pp66-68.

185 Gartenstein-Ross, "When Muslims Convert", pp66-68.

186 Najjar, "Islamic Fundamentalism and the Intellectuals: The Case of Naguib Mahfouz", *British Journal of Middle Eastern Studies*, Vol. 25, No. 1, May 1998, pp139-168; Ami Ayalon, "Egypt's Quest for Cultural Orientation", *The Moshe Dayan Center for Middle Eastern and African Studies*, Tel Aviv University, 1999, http://www.dayan.org/D&A-Egypt-ami.htm.

187 Najjar, "Islamic Fundamentalism", pp177-200.

188 The *sunna* are the actions of Muhammad in his lifetime, his perfect, personal example, normative for all Muslims.

189 Fiona Lloyd-Davies, "No Compromise", *BBC News*, 26 October 2001, http://news.bbc.co.uk/1/hi/programmes/correspondent/1619902.stm; "Egypt", *Amnesty International Report 2002*, AI Index: POL 10/001/2002; Philip Smucker, "Lawyer Calls for Divorce over 'insult to Islam'", *Electronic Telegraph*, 25 April 2001; "Egyptian 'infidel' case dismissed", *BBC News*, Middle East, 30 July 2001, http://news.bbc.co.uk/1/hi/world/middle_east/1464549.stm.

190 Ahmed, "Pakistan's Blasphemy Law", pB01; Barry Bearak, "Death to Blasphemers: Islam's Grip on Pakistan", *New York Times*, Foreign Desk, Late edition, 12 May 2001, Section A, p3; "Pakistan doctor faces death for blasphemy", CNN.com, 20 August 2001; Susannah Price, "Pakistani sentenced to death for blasphemy", *BBC News Online: World: South Asia*, 18 August 2001, http://news.bbc.co.uk/1/low/world/south_asia/1498121.stm; Susannah Price, "Pakistani appeals over death sentence", *BBC News Online: World: South Asia*, 21 August 2001, http://news.bbc.co.uk/1/low/world/south_asia/1502650.stm; Amnesty International News Release, "Blasphemy Laws Should Be Abolished", 21 August 2001, http://www.amnestyusa.org/news/2001/pakistan08212001.html.

191 "Abdollah Nouri, Prisoner of Conscience , Iran", *Amnesty International, Medical Action*, AI Index: MDE13/010/2002; John F. Burns, "Iran Hard-Liners Try Cleric, Who Tries Them", *New York Times*, Foreign Desk, 10 November 1999; John F. Burns, "Court Silences Iran Reformist With Jail Term", *New York Times*, 28 November 1999; "Iran: Abdollah Nouri's Release Welcomed, But All Prisoners of Conscience Must also Be Released", *Amnesty International On-Line*, 6 November

2002, AI Index: MDE 13/020/2002, http://www.amnesty.org/ai.nsf/print/ MDE130202002?OpenDocument.

192 An Open Letter to Ayatollah Hashemi-Shahroudi from Human Rights Watch; "Iran: Prosecution of Independent Clerk Condemned", *Human Rights Watch*, 11 October 2000, http://www.hrw.org/press/2000/10/iran1010.htm; "Iran: Amnesty International Report 2002", *Amnesty International*, AI Index: POL 10/001/2002; Sadeq Saba, "Liberal Iranian Cleric Jailed", *BBC News*, Monday, 14 October 2002, http://news.bbc.co.uk/1/hi/world/middle_east/2327499.stm.

193 Ali Akbar Dareini, "Scholar Sentenced to Death in Iran", Associated Press; Joe Stork, "Iran: Academic's Death Sentence Condemned", *Human Rights Watch*, http://www.hrw.org/press/2002/11/iranacademic.htm; "Protests Grow In Iran Over Death Sentence for Professor", *Human Rights Monitor*, 12 November 2002, http://www.humanrightsmonitor.org/article601.html; Ayelet Savyon, "The Call for Islamic Protestantism: Dr. Hashem Aghajari's Speech and Subsequent Death Sentence", *MEMRI Special Dispatch Series*, No. 445, 2 December 2002, http://memri.org/bin/opener.cgi?Page=archives&ID=SP44502.

194 Ali Akbar Dareini, "Iranian professor freed from jail in Tehran", *The Guardian*, 2 August 2004.

195 "Government Should Ensure Safety of Taslima Nasrin", *Amnesty International Public Statement*, Bangladesh, 14 October 1998, AI Index: ASA 13/01/98; "Taslima goes back into exile", *BBC News Online*, World: South Asia, 26 January 1999, http://news.bbc.co.uk/1/low/world/south_asia/263014.stm; "Bangladesh Police hunt feminist writer", *BBC News Online: World: South Asia*, 25 September 1998.

196 Jack Malvern, "Chapter and verse for novel protests", *TimesOnline*, 21 October 2002; "20th anniversary of fatwa for author Salman Rushdie", *The MEMRI Blog*, http://www.thememriblog.org/blog_personal/en/13700.htm (viewed 8 April 2009).

197 Genevieve Abdo, "Khomeini Threat Lives On", *The Guardian*, 12 February 1999, http://www.guardian.co.uk/Print/0,3858,3820765,00.html.

198 Andrew Osborn, "Woman in hiding after she lambasts Islam", *The Observer*, 6 October 2002; Marlise Simons, "Behind the Veil: A Muslim Woman Speaks Out", *New York Times*, Foreign Desk, The Saturday Profile, Late Edition – Final, 9 November 2002, Section A , Page 4, Column 3.

199 Dean E. Murphy, "Jordanian Muslim Cleric Calls for Death of Author in the U.S.", *New York Times*, 30 June 2001.

200 "Iran, Religious and Ethnic Minorities: Discrimination in Law and in Practice", *Human Rights Watch*, http://www.hrw.org/reports/1997/iran/Iran-05.html.

201 "Excerpts from Amnesty International Report, ASA 33/10/94, Pakistan", http://www.thepersecution.org/amnst194.html; "Pakistan: Insufficient Protection of Religious

Minorities", *Amnesty International*, May 2001, AI Index: ASA 33/008/2001.

202 Ardeshir Cowasjee, "Fellow-man", *DAWN*, Internet Edition, 20 August 2000, http://www.dawn.com/weekly/cowas/20000820.htm; "Individual Case Reports: Mirza Mbarak Ahmad Nusrat", http://www.thepersecution.org/case001.html.

203 "Plight of Ahmadi Muslims in Pakistan (1989-1999)", http://www.thepersecution. org/archive/pl_blaw.html.

204 Malvern, "Chapter and verse"; Charles Bremer, "Author cleared of inciting religious hatred", *TimesOnline*, 23 October 2002.

205 Malvern, "Chapter and verse"; Rod Dreher, "Oriana's Screed", *National Review Online*, 8 October 2002, http://www.nationalreview.com/dreher/dreher101002.asp.

206 Malvern, "Chapter and verse"; "An Intellectual Catastrophe", *Al-Ahram Weekly On-line*, Issue No. 389, 6-12 August, 1998, http://www.ahram.org.eg/ weekly/1998/389/cu1.htm; Geoffrey Wheatcroft, "A Terrifying Honesty", *The Atlantic Monthly* (Books & Critics), February 2002, http://www.theatlantic.com/ issues/2002/02/wheatcroft.htm.

207 *Contra* W. Heffening, "Murtadd", in Gibb and Kramers, *Shorter Encyclopaedia of Islam*, p413; see Siddiqi, *The Penal Law of Islam*, p109, where he states: "There is almost complete consensus of opinion among the jurists that apostasy from Islam (Irtidad) must be punished by death."

208 An example of incitement to mob violence based on a false accusation of blasphemy (Christians were falsely accused of tearing and burning pages of the Qur'an, as well as of writing blasphemous statements on them) is documented in Sookhdeo, *A People Betrayed*, pp268-274. Large mobs of infuriated Muslims led by clerics and armed with sticks, axes, knives, firearms, explosives and petrol bombs attacked the Christians in the village of Shanti Nagar in the Punjab, Pakistan, on 5 and 6 February 1997, looting houses and setting them on fire and destroying telephone and electricity connections and water supplies. A number of Christian women were abducted.

Index

The Arabic definite article (al-) at the beginning of an entry is ignored for purposes of alphabetisation.

Notes are indicated by 'n' after the page number, e.g., 'Umar (Caliph) 117(n8)

'Abbasids 42, 123–124
'Abd al-Karim Mal al-Allah 65
'Abd Al-Muta'al Al-Sa'idi 126–127
Al-Abdari Ibn-Ḥadj, Mohammed 30
Abdu, Muhammad 126
Abdullah 23
'Abdur-Raziq 104, 105
Abu Bakr (Caliph) 22, 41, 121–122, 123
Abu Bakr al-Farsi al-Shafi'i 47
Abu Bakr al-Mundhir 48
Abu Dawud 23, 25–26
Abu Hanbali 47
    see also Hanbali School
Abu Hanifa 47
    see also Hanafi School
Abu Hurairah 103
Abu Musa 26, 104

Abu Sa'id al-Khudri 26
Abu Shuja' al-Isfahani 34–35
Abu 'Umar Ash-Shaybani 104
Abu-Qilaba 23
Abu-Zayd, Nasr Hamid 85–87, 125
Abu'l Mus'ab 39, 48
adat (local customary law) 71
Afghanistan 80–81, 108
Aghajari, Hashem 90–91
ahad 111–115
    see also hadith
Ahmad ibn Hanbal 37, 48
Ahmad ibn Naqib al-Misri,
    'Umdat al-Salik (*The Reliance of the Traveller*) 34, 36
Ahmad, Nasir 96–97
Ahmad of Qadian, Ghulam 95
Ahmadis 65–66, 95–96, 125
Ahmed, Akbar S. 65–66
'A'ishah 113
Al-Hurriyyah al-Dimiyyah fi al-Islam (*Freedom of Religion in Islam*) (Abd Al-Muta'al Al-Sa'idi) 126–127
Ali, Ayyan Hirsi 93
Ali Gomaa 51

'Ali ibn Abi Talib 25, 47, 103
'Ali, Yusuf 18
'Alier, Abel 77
Alladin Omer Ajjabna
    Mohammed 76–77
Allah
    Islamic concept of 50
    and justification for punishment
        106–107, 110–111, 113
Allawi, Ali A. 50
analogy (*qiyas*) 15, 21, 27
Anas 105
al-Anbiyya 116
anti-apostasy organisations 64
apostasy
    amendments to apostasy law
        51–53
    blasphemy and heresy as 46–50
    definitions of 30, 33–34,
        37–38 , 49–50, 123–124
    deviation from Islamic
        orthodoxy 85–92
    hidden 115–116
    ideological guidelines for
        judging 109–111
    jurists' discretionary powers on
        65, 70, 111
    major and minor 8, 104–106
    reasons for 17–18
    of rulers 114–115
    as threat to Islam 101–104,
        106–108
    as treason 8, 42–44, 100, 123
    see also blasphemy; converts;
        death penalty; legal systems;
        punishments; shari'a
"Apostasy: Major and Minor" (al-
    Qaradawi) 101–118

Article 18, UDHR 10, 14, 61,
    100, 119, 124, 132
asylum 79, 81, 89, 132, 142
Australia, Department of
    Immigration and Citizenship
    52
El-'Awa, Mohamed S. 42, 49
Awlad Haritna (*Children of our
    Quarter*) (Mahfouz) 85
Al-Azhar university, Cairo 8, 19,
    44, 68, 86, 125

Babul, Zainal Abedin 92
Badawi, Abdullah 72
Badawi, Zaki 42, 49
    "Freedom of Religion in Islam"
        119–127
Baha'is 94–95, 126
Baidhawi, 20
al-Baihaqi 105
Bangladesh 91–92
al-Baqarah 106, 107
Battle of Uhud (625 A.D.)
    20–21, 24
belief *see* religious freedom;
    unbelief
Beyond Belief (Naipaul) 97–98
Bhutto, Benazir 66–67
blasphemy
    against Muhammad 9–10,
        46–47, 65, 88, 90–91
    and heresy 46–50
    and non-Muslims 58–63
    see also death penalty; defama-
        tion; legal systems; Penal
        Code; punishments; shari'a
Blasphemy Law, Pakistan (Penal
    Code) 9, 49, 65–67, 125

case studies of 79–80, 88,
     95–97
British Muslims, converts to
     Christianity 83–84
al-Bukhari 22–26, 115
burial, of apostates 24–25, 45

Cairo Declaration on Human
     Rights 10, 50–51
Caliphs 121–122
     see also 'Umar
capital punishment see death
     penalty
censorship 68
children, of apostates 31, 35,
     37–38, 109
     in present-day Islamic nations
     67, 74–75, 81
Children of Abraham (Duran)
     93–94
Children of our Quarter (Awlad
     Haritna) (Mahfouz) 85
choice, freedom of 50, 56–58
Christians/Christianity
     apostasy/converts to 33, 39,
     63–65, 74–84
     blasphemy charges against
     65–66
     Christian mission 63–64, 102
     Islamic state recognition of 70
     Muhammad's attitude to 121
     relations with Islam 10–11
     shari'a incompatible with 27
     Western support for Muslim
     converts 80
     see also minority groups;
     non-Muslims
civil rights, loss of 75, 124–125

Classical Commentary on the Holy
     Qur'an (Tafsir al-Qurtubi) 21
clerics (Hojatolislam) 89–90
colonialism 115
communism 102, 108
compulsion
     and punishment 21–22
     in religion 41
     to apostasy 37
consensus see ijma'
constitutions
     Afghanistan 81
     Egypt 67–68, 125
     family law 120
     Iran 70–71, 95
     Kuwait 76
     Malaysia 71–72, 82
     Maldives 73
     Pakistan 95
     Saudi Arabia 55, 64–65
     Sudan 69–70
     see also Blasphemy Law,
     Pakistan; Cairo Declaration
     on Human Rights; civil
     rights; freedom; human
     rights; UDHR
converts
     in Britain 83–84
     in Muslim-majority countries
     73–82
     to/from Islamic sectarian
     groups 94–97
criminal law
     secular 75
     shari'a 16
     see also shari'a
Crisis of Islamic Civilization
     (Allawi) 50

Dar al-Iftaa 51–52
death penalty
  for blasphemy 47–48, 58–59,
    65
  hadithic support for 16,
    22–27, 42, 46–47, 52–53,
    103–104, 111–115
  for major apostasy 8, 105
  methods of execution 39
  Muslim opposition to 42, 51,
    122
  in present-day Muslim states
    65, 68, 70–72, 124
    for Christian converts 63,
      75, 77–79
    for converts to/from Islamic
      sectarian groups 95
    individual cases 88, 90, 125
  present-day reassessment of 127
  Qur'an has no mention of 8,
    19, 42, 52, 111
  Qur'anic support for asserted
    16, 20–22, 107, 122
  refutation of objections to
    111–115
  scholars' discussions of 41–53,
    99
  shari'a law on 7–9, 27, 37,
    56–58, 122–123
    Hanafi School 30, 31
    Hanbali School 37
    Maliki School 32–33
    Shafi'i School 34, 35–36
    summary of sentences 28–29
  see also hudud offences; legal
    systems; punishments; shari'a
death threats 81–85, 92–93
  and disappearances of

Christian converts 65, 78, 80
  see also fatwas; persecution
defamation
  "insult" to Islam 70, 86–87,
    91–92, 125
  ISC resolution on 59–61
  UN resolution on 62–63
  see also blasphemy
dhimmi see non-Muslims
Dibaj, Mehdi 77–78
discretionary punishments *see*
  ta'zir offences
discrimination, ISC resolution on
  59–61
divorce *see* marriage, separation
  and divorce
double talk 52
  taqiyya 94
drunkenness 31–32, 36–37
Duran, Khalid 93–94

edicts 93–94
Egypt 51–52, 67–68, 85–87, 125
  Al-Azhar university 8, 19, 44,
    68, 86, 125
"The Enlightenment" organisation 88
equality, constitutional 67
Eshkevari, Hassan Youssef 89–90
estate, inheritance of *see* property
execution, methods of 39
  see also death penalty
exile 85, 89, 92, 143
extremist organisations 88, 91, 93

FAKTA (Forum Against
  Conversion Movement) 64
Fallaci, Oriana 97

families, of converts 57, 65,
    74–75, 81, 83–84
family law 120
fatwas 57, 63, 66–68, 89, 92, 109
    see also death threats; persecution
female apostates
    Hanafi ruling on 122
    present day cases 65, 71,
        81–82, 87, 91–92
    punishment of 7, 24, 31–32,
        35, 37–38
fiqh (Islamic law) 7, 53, 68
    see also Schools of Law; shari‘a
Forum Against Conversion
    Movement (FAKTA) 64
freedom
    of choice 50, 56–58
    and compulsion 41
    of converts to Christianity
        74–84
    and predestination 123
    of speech 61–62, 87, 91
    of thought and expression 61,
        100
    see also Cairo Declaration on
        Human Rights; civil rights;
        freedom; human rights;
        religious freedom; UDHR
Freedom of Religion in Islam
    (*Al-Hurriyyah al-Dimiyyah
    fi al-Islam*) (Abd Al-Muta'al
    Al-Sa'idi) 126–127
Freedom of Religion in Islam
    (Badawi) 119–127
freethinkers *see* heresy; *zindiqs*
fundamentalism *see* Islamism;
    modernist views; Qaradawi,
    Yusuf; traditionalist views

Gayoom, Maumoon Abdul 73
Ghanoushi, Shaikh 127
al-Ghazali, Sheik Muhammad
    68, 126
al-Ghazari, Ibrahim 39
Gibb, H. 19
God, Islamic concept of 50
    see also Allah
grandchildren of apostates 31,
    35, 37–38
Guided Caliphs 121–122

hadd offences *see hudud* offences
hadith
    claims to divine authority 15, 41
    on punishments for apostasy
        7, 9, 22–27, 42, 46–47,
        103–104
    support for death penalty 16,
        52–53, 111–115
Haider, Farooq 97
Hamadi, Mullah Ahmad Mian 96
Hanafi School 28–31, 122
    see also Abu Hanifa
Hanbali School 28–29, 37–38
Hedaya 30–31
heresy 46–50
    heretics 32–33, 37, 70, 110,
        124
    sectarian groups 70, 74, 94–97
hidden apostasy 115–116
Hindus 91–92
hisba 68, 86–87
Hojatolislam (clerics) 89–90
"honour crimes" 65
Houellbecq, Michel 97
hudud offences (singular *hadd*)
    16, 27, 49, 99

Al-Azhar University's views on
44
blasphemy as 48
hadith basis of 22
Hanafi law on 30
in Malaysia 72
Shafi'i law on 33–34
Shi'a law on 38
see also death penalty; *ta'zir*
offences
human rights 50–51, 56–58,
59–63, 100
see also Cairo Declaration on
Human Rights; civil rights;
freedom; UDHR
Al-Hurriayat Al'Am Fi Al-Daula
Al-Islamiyya (Ghanoushi) 127
Hussein, Nissar 83–84
hypocrites 20–21, 33, 41, 110,
113–114, 116

'ibadat (rituals) 15
Ibn Abbas, Malik 22, 24–25, 48,
103
Ibn Abi Uways 48
Ibn Hanbal 37, 48
Ibn Hazm 105
Ibn Mas'ud 103–104, 107
Ibn Rajab 103
Ibn Taymiyah 8, 42, 104–106, 113
As-Sarim Al-Maslul 'ala Shatim
Ar-Rasul 110
Ibn Wahb 48
Ibn Warraq 39
Ibrahim, Haris Mohamed 72
identity, Islamic 42–46, 68, 76,
106–108, 115
and conversion 83

ideological guidelines, for judging
apostasy 109–111
IIFA (International Islamic Fiqh
Academy) 53
ijma' (consensus) 15, 21, 27, 34–35
al-Qaradawi on 105, 109–113
ijtihad (application of reason) 10,
21, 27, 110
Ikrima 22
Imami-Shi'i School *see* Ja'fari
School
imprisonment
of converts to Christianity
77–81
of Muslims 89–91, 96–97, 122
of non-Muslims in Muslim
states 125
aal 'Imran 107
incitement to racial hatred
60–62, 97, 144
the individual 50–51, 61
official status of 82
see also identity, Islamic
Indonesia 64
inheritance
of apostates' properties and
estates 31, 33
by apostates 75
"insult" to Islam 9, 70, 86–87,
91–92, 97–98, 125
intellectuals
Al-Qaradawi's refutation of
111–114
intellectual apostasy 115–116
Muslim 68, 74, 85–94, 110–
111, 124–126
in the West 63, 92–94
see also fiqh; jurists; modernist

views; scholars, Islamic;
  traditionalist views
International Islamic Fiqh
  Academy (IIFA) 53
Iqbal, Tahir 79–80
Iran 70–71, 77–78, 89–91,
  94–95, 126
irtidad (apostate) 16
  see also apostasy
Islam
  converts from, to Christianity
    in Muslim states 74–82
    in the West 82–84
  deviations from orthodoxy
    85–92
  early apostasy rulings 49
  reform of 10, 88–90
  relations with Christians
    10–11
  sectarian groups in 70, 74,
    94–97
  as state religion 64–65,
    67–68,
    70–73
  Western views of 53
  see also Muslim states; Muslims;
    Qur'an; shari'a
ul-Islam, Zia 67
Al Islam 'Akida wa Sharia
  (Shaltout) 126
Islamic Summit Conference
  (Dakar 2008) 59–61
Islamism
  definition of apostasy 50
  extremist organisations 88, 91,
    93
  growth of 55, 57–58, 65–68,
    72, 86–87

view of shari'a 46
Islamophobia 60–61, 97
Istitabah 122
  see also repentance

Ja'fari School 16, 27–29
Jews/Judaism 39, 70, 93, 121
jihad 64, 108
Joy, Lina 81–82
judgments, guidelines for
  109–111
jurists 19–27, 33–39, 41–53,
  101–116, 122–125
  see also Abu Shuja' al-Isfahani;
    fiqh; *ijma'*; intellectuals;
    Mawdudi, Abul A'la;
    modernist views; Qadi
    'Iyad; Qaradawi, Yusuf;
    scholars, Islamic; Siddiqi,
    Muhammad Iqbal;
    traditionalist views

Khamenei, Ayatollah 91
al-Khazan 19
Khomeini, Ayatollah 92, 95
killers, of apostates, punishments
  for 31, 36–37
Kramer, J. 19
kufr (unbelief) 42, 45–46, 49,
  79, 86–87
Kuku, Mekki 77
Kurdi, Abdurahman Abdulkadir
  43
Kuwait, converts from Islam
  74–75

Lajja (*Shame*) (Nasrin) 91–92
law *see fiqh*; Schools of Law

legal actions, against converts
75–84
legal systems
manipulation of 66–67, 72
secular and shari'a 55, 66–67,
71–72, 75
see also apostasy; blasphemy;
death penalty; punishments;
Schools of Law; shari'a
liberal views 45, 74, 76, 86–87,
100
see also intellectuals; modernist
views

al-Mabsut (Ibn Kinana) 39, 48, 103
madhahib (school of law) see
Hanafi School; Hanbali
School; Ja'fari School; Maliki
School; Schools of Law; Shafi'i
School
Al Madkhal (Mohammed
Al-Abdari Ibn-Hadj) 30
Mahfouz, Naguib 86, 125
Awlad Haritna (Children of our
Quarter) 85
Mahmassani, Subhi 42
Mahrami, Zabibullah 94–95
al-Ma'idah 106, 113
Malaysia 71–72, 81–82
Maldives 72–74
Malik, al-Muwatta 26–27
Malik ibn Abbas 22, 24–25, 48, 103
Malik, Safdar Hussain 88
Maliki School 28–29, 31–33,
47–48
marriage, separation and divorce
(of apostates) 19, 31, 33, 38,
45, 67, 109

court orders ignored 125
Muslim/Christian marriages 82
present day cases 68, 74–75,
81, 85–87
wives as apostates 31, 83
see also female apostates; women
Masih, Ashiq (Kingri) 80
Mawdudi, Abul A'la 16, 19–20,
43
mental illness 33, 36–37, 81
Minhaj-at-Taliban (Nawawi) 33,
35
minority groups
in Muslim states 63, 65–66,
68, 70–71, 73
sectarian 70, 74, 94–97
see also Christians/Christianity;
Jews/Judaism; non-Mus-
lims; Zoroastrianism
minors 30, 35, 37
see also children
Mishkat al Masabih 23
modernist views
death penalty 42
Islamisation 72
punishment 17, 19, 22, 42
reform of apostasy law 51
shari'a law 45–46
see also intellectuals;
traditionalist views
Mohamad, Mahathir 72
Mu'adh 104
mu'amallat (social relations) 15
Mu'awiyah ibn Haidah 103
Muhammad
blasphemy against 46–47, 65,
88, 90–91
death penalty for apostasy

authorised by 22–24, 26,
    41, 103–104, 121
death penalty for political
    betrayal authorised by 42
wars of 120–121
al-Mujadilah 113
Mukhtasar fil Risalah (Abu Shuja'
    al-Isfahani) 34–35
munafiqun 20–21
murtadd (apostate) 16, 44, 58
    see also apostasy
Musharraf, Pervez 67
Muslim, Sahih 25, 115
Muslim Australians (Saeed) 52–53
Muslim Brotherhood 93
Muslim states
    blasphemy and non-Muslims
        58–63, 65–66
    converts from Islam to
        Christianity 74–82
    death penalty in 65, 68,
        70–72, 88, 90, 124–125
    individual state practices
        64–74
    non-Muslims (*dhimmi*) in
        65–68, 70–71, 73, 125
    shari'a in 55–58
    see also Cairo Declaration
        of Human Rights; Islam;
        Islamism; Organization of
        the Islamic Conference
Muslims
    blasphemy charges against
        66–67
    converts from Islam 74–82
    and threat of apostasy 101–
        104, 106–108
    see also Islam; Islamism

al-Mustawrad Al-'Ajli 104
al-Mutairi, Fatima 65

al-Nahda Party, Tunisia 127
Naipaul, Sir Vidia S. 97–98
al-Nakhi, Ibrahim 42, 105, 112,
    122
Nasheed, Mohamed 73–74
Nasrin, Taslima 91–92
nationality, loss of 75
Nawawi, 33, 35
Niazi, Mawlana Abadu Sitar 66
NIF (National Islamic Front),
    Sudan 77
an-Nisaa' 110, 111
non-Muslims
    and blasphemy 46–50, 58–63,
        65–66
    conversion to Islam 83
    and insults to Islam 97–98, 125
    in Muslim states 65–68,
        70–71, 73, 125
    rights of 55–56
    targetting of 74
    see also Christians/Christianity;
        Jews/Judaism; Zoroastrianism
Nouri, Abdollah 89
an-Nur 111
Nusrat, Mirza Mubarak Ahmad
    95–96

Obama, Barack 13
OIC 51, 60–63
Omar, Muhammad Haj 78–79
Organization of the Islamic
    Conference 51, 60–63
orthodox Islam, deviation from
    85–92

Pakistan 62–63, 65–67, 79–80,
    88–89, 95–97, 125
    see also Blasphemy Law,
        Pakistan
paradise, as reward for killing
    apostates 25
PAS (Islamist Party of Malaysia) 72
penal codes
    Egypt 67–68
    Iran (Theologians' Law) 70, 95
    see also blasphemy; Blasphemy
        Law, Pakistan; death penalty;
        defamation; *hudud* offences;
        punishments; shari'a; *ta'zir*
        offences
The Penal Law of Islam (Siddiqi)
    16, 19–20, 43–44
penalties *see* death penalty; *hudud*
    offences; imprisonment; legal
    systems; persecution; punish-
    ments; shari'a; *ta'zir* offences;
    torture
persecution
    of Christian converts in the
        West 82–84
    of Muslim intellectuals 85–89,
        124–126
    see also asylum; death penalty;
        death threats; exile; impris-
        onment; torture
personal disputes, and blasphe-
    my charges 9, 66–67, 79, 88,
    99–100
political contexts
    of apostasy 49, 51, 123–124
    apostasy of rulers 114–115
    of dispute and blasphemy
        charges 66–67

of Islam 41–44
Pourmand, Hamid 78
predestination, doctrine of 123
prescribed punishments *see hudud*
    offences
prison *see* imprisonment
property, of apostates 31, 33,
    36–37, 67, 124–125
The Punishment of the Apostate
    According to Islamic Law
    (Mawdudi) 16, 19–20, 43
punishments 16–17, 19, 102–104
    basic penalties for apostasy 99
    for blasphemy and heresy
        46–47
    for female apostates 122
    hadithic teachings on 7, 9,
        22–27, 42, 46–47, 103–104
    Hanafi rules on 30–31
    Hanbali rules on 37–38
    Maliki rules on 31–33
    modernist views on 17, 19,
        22, 42
    in present-day Muslim states
        56–58, 65, 67–68, 70–71,
        73, 85–92
    Qur'anic teachings on 7–8,
        17–27, 52, 107–108
    reasons for severity of 106–108
    responsibility for 109–111
    Shafi'i rules on 33–37
    traditionalist views on 16–17,
        19–21
    see also death penalty; *hudud*
        offences; imprisonment;
        legal systems; persecution;
        shari'a; *ta'zir* offences; torture

Qadi 'Iyad 39, 58–59
    Ash Shifa 47–48
Qadri, Anwar Ahmad, A Sunni
    Shafi'i Law Code 34–35
Qambar, Hussein Ali 74–76
al-Qaradawi, Yusuf 8, 45
    Apostasy: Major and Minor
    101–118
al-Qayrawani, 'Abdullah ibn Abi
    Zayd, Al-Risala 32–33
qiyas (analogy) 15, 21, 27
Qur'an 15–27, 37
    on blasphemy 58–59
    on compulsion in religion 41
    criticism of by non-Muslims 97
    desecrations of as crime 65,
        79, 86–87
    doctrine of creation of 124
    and freedom of religion 126
    no support for death penalty
        8, 19, 42, 52, 111
    and prophetic traditions 120
    as state constitution 55
    support for death penalty 16,
        20–22, 107, 122
    teachings on punishment 7–8,
        52, 107–108
al-Qurtubi, Tafsir al-Qurtubi
    (Classical Commentary on the
    Holy Qur'an) 21

La Rabbia e L'Orgoglio (Rage and
    Pride) (Fallaci) 97
ar-Ra'd 116
Rage and Pride (La Rabbia e
    L'Orgoglio) (Fallaci) 97
Rahman, Abdul 80–81
Ramadan, Tariq 27

reason
    analogical (qiyas) 15, 21, 27
    application of (ijtihad) 10, 21,
        27, 110
recantation 122
    see also repentance
reform
    of apostasy law 51–52
    of Islam 10, 88–90
The Reliance of the Traveller
    ('Umdat al-Salik) (Ahmad ibn
    Naqib al-Misri) 34, 36
religious freedom
    Islamic restriction of other
        religions 63–64, 70–71,
        73–74
    Islamic understanding of 56,
        75, 81, 100, 126–127
    Qur'anic support for 120–
        122, 126
    and shari'a 10, 75, 81
    see also Cairo Declaration on
        Human Rights; civil rights;
        freedom; human rights;
        UDHR; unbelief
religious minorities see Christians/
    Christianity; Jews/Judaism;
    minority groups; non-Mus-
    lims; Zoroastrianism
renunciation see repentance
repeat apostasy 37
repentance (taubah) 25–27, 43,
    104–105, 110–111, 122
    Al-Azhar recommendation on
        8, 68
    Hanafi rules on 30
    Hanbali rules on 37
    Maliki rules on 32

rehabilitation in Malaysian
states 72
Shafi'i rules on 34–35
rewards, for killing apostates 25
ridda (apostasy) 16, 34
see also apostasy
Ridda Wars 22, 41
Ridha, Rashid 126
rights see Cairo Declaration on
Human Rights; civil rights;
freedom; human rights; religious freedom; UDHR
Al-Risala (al-Qayrawani) 32–33
rituals ('ibadat) 15
rulers, apostasy of 114–115
Rushdie, Salman, *The Satanic
Verses* 92

al-Sa'adawi, Nawwal 87
Sabir, Peerzada 'Ali Ahmed 79, 80
sacred–secular dichotomy 42–43,
55, 58–64, 102, 119
see also modernist views;
Westernisation
Saeed, Abdullah, *Muslim
Australians* 52
Saeed, Abdullah and Hassan 46,
52–53, 64, 73
al Samad, Muhammad Samida
'Abd 86
*As-Sarim Al-Maslul 'ala Shatim
Ar-Rasul* (Ibn Taymiyah) 110
The Satanic Verses (Rushdie) 92
Saudi Arabia 55, 64–65
scholarly consensus see *ijma'*
scholars, Islamic
definition of apostasy 49
interpretations of Islamic texts 99

issue of *fatwas* 109
see also Abu Shuja' al-Isfahani;
Badawi, Zaki; *fiqh*; intellectuals; jurists; Mawdudi,
Abul A'la; modernist views;
Qadi 'Iyad; Qaradawi,
Yusuf; Siddiqi, Muhammad
Iqbal; traditionalist views
Schools of Law 7, 120
see also Hanafi School; Hanbali
School; Ja'fari School; Maliki
School; Shafi'i School
sectarian groups 70, 74, 94–97
secular-liberalism 86–87
see also intellectuals; liberal
views; modernist views
secular–sacred dichotomy 42–43,
55, 58–64, 102, 119
see also modernist views;
Westernisation
separation see marriage, separation
and divorce
al-Shafi'i, Abu Bakr al-Farsi 47
Shafi'i School 28–29, 33–37, 47
Shah, Hannah 84
Shahin, 'Abd al-Sabur 86
Shahroudi, Mahmoud Hashemi
91
Shaikh, Muhammad Younus
88–89
Shaltout, Mahmud 126
Shame (*Lajja*) (Nasrin) 91–92
shari'a 15, 27–38
blasphemy rules 47–48
crimes against God 16
on death penalty 7–9, 27, 37,
56–58, 122–123
Hanafi School 30, 31

Hanbali School 37
Maliki School 32–33
Shafi'i School 34–36
and freedom of religion 10,
75, 81
fundamentalist views on 46,
111–112
and human rights 51, 62
modernist views on 45–46
new interpretations of 126–127
and state constitutions 8,
55–57, 64–65, 67–71, 99
Syariah law 71–72, 82
see also death penalty; hudud
offences; legal systems;
punishments
Shi'a Islam 27, 38, 70, 94
Ja'fari School 16, 27–29
Ash Shifa (Qadi 'Iyad) 47–48
Shorter Encyclopaedia of Islam
(Gibb and Kramer) 19
Siddiqi, Muhammad Iqbal 16,
19–20, 43–44
Sisters in Islam 72
social order, Islamic 42–46, 68,
76, 90
social penalties 57, 66, 82–84
social relations (mu'amallat) 15
Soodmand, Hossein 77
speech, freedom of 61–62, 87, 91
the state see Muslim states; non-
Muslims; rulers; secular–sacred
dichotomy; Westernisation
status
of individual 82
of women 90, 92–93
Sudan 69–70, 76–77, 126
Sunni Islam

laws on apostasy 30
in Maldives 73
see also Hanafi School; Hanbali
School; Maliki School;
Shafi'i School
A Sunni Shafi'i Law Code (Qadri)
34–35
suras 17
see also Qur'an
Syariah law 71–72, 82
see also shari'a

Tabari 124
Tafsir al-Qurtubi (Classical
Commentary on the Holy
Qur'an) 21
Taha, Mahmud Muhammad 126
takfir 49, 68
Tantawi, Sheik Mohammed
Sayyed 13, 51
taqiyya 94
double talk 52
taubah (repentance) see repentance
at-Tawbah 113
ta'zir offences 27, 32, 35, 37, 42,
99
blasphemy as 46, 48
see also hudud offences;
punishments
ath-Thawri 105, 112
al-Tirmidhi 23
Tori, Ghorban 78
torture 39, 68, 76–78, 124
UDHR on 130, 143
traditionalist views
on death penalty 41–45, 53
and deviations from orthodoxy
85–87

on punishment 16–17, 19–22
on reform of apostasy law
    51–52
on shari'a 46
see also intellectuals; modern-
    ist views; Qaradawi, Yusuf;
    Westernisation
treason, apostasy as 8, 42–44,
    100, 123
al-Turabi, Hassan 126

UDHR 50, 76, 119
    Article 18: 10, 14, 61, 100,
        119, 124, 132
    full text of 129–144
Uhud, Battle of (625 A.D.)
    20–21, 24
Umar Barakat, Sheikh 34
'Umar (or Omar) (Caliph) 8,
    26–27, 39, 104–105, 117(n8),
    122
Umayyads 42
'Umdat al-Salik (*The Reliance
    of the Traveller*) (Ahmad ibn
    Naqib al-Misri) 34, 36
umma 8, 76, 100
unbelief (*kufr*) 42, 45–46, 49,
    79, 86–87
UNHRC 60–63
United Kingdom 83–84
United Nations Human Rights
    Council *see* UNHRC
Universal Declaration of Human
    Rights *see* UDHR
USA 84
'Utbah ibn Farqad 104
'Uthman Ibn Kinana 39, 48, 103

Wahhabis 64
al-Wahsh, Nabil 87
wars 20–21, 105–106, 120–122
    of Apostasy 122–123
    Ridda Wars 22, 41
Westernisation 53, 55, 102, 115,
    124
    see also Christians/Christianity;
        intellectuals; modernist
        views; UDHR; UNHRC
women' rights and status 90,
    92–93
    see also female apostates;
        marriage; Sisters in Islam
writers *see* intellectuals; jurists;
    scholars, Islamic

Yemen 78–79
Yousef, Sheikh Ali 125

Zakat 123
Zaki, Y. 42–43
Zant, Sheik Abdul Moneim Abu
    93
zindiqs (or *zendiqs*) 32, 110, 124
    see also heresy
Zoroastrianism 70, 121
Zwemer, S. 20, 41